# I'M SORRY

# SORRY
## I DIDN'T
## MEAN TO

# AND OTHER **LIES**
## WE LOVE TO TELL

# I'M SORRY I DIDN'T MEAN TO

## AND OTHER LIES WE LOVE TO TELL

### Jerald M. Jellison, Ph.D.

**Chatham Square Press**
**New York**

Published by Chatham Square Press
401 Broadway, New York, N.Y. 10013

**Library of Congress Cataloging in Publication Data**

Jellison, Jerald M        1942–
    I'm sorry, I didn't mean to, and other lies we love to
tell.

        1. Interpersonal    relations.    2. Truthfulness    and
falsehood.    I.    Title.
HM132.J39            158'.2            77-10125
ISBN 0-89456-005-0


Printing 123456789
Printed in the United States of America

Distributed by Contemporary Books, Inc.
180 North Michigan Avenue, Chicago, Ill. 60601

To My Parents

# Acknowledgments

I want to thank the following people for their constructive comments on an earlier, more technical version of this work: Robert Arkin, Kevin Gentry, Clyde Hendrick, Edward E. Jones, Wendy Martyna, Judson Mills, Cheri Rozsa, Sylvia Stern, Carol Warren, and Elizabeth Wheeler. Peggy Jellison deserves thanks for the valuable assistance she provided throughout this project. Finally I want to express my gratitude to Chuck Adams, whose editorial assistance so substantially contributed to the quality of this work.

# Contents

# Preface

Yes, this is a self-help book. And, yes, it is about lies.

Unlike some other self-help books, however, it claims no miracle cure, it does not announce the diagnosis of a new psychological pathology, and it does not insist that you institute drastic therapeutic changes. And while the goals of this volume are several (and lofty), they are not bombastic, nor is the tone intended to be strident. Rather you are asked simply to look at your own behavior and at the games you play with others—all others, from strangers to loved ones. By *recognizing* what it is you are doing, and by *acknowledging* that you are doing it, you are well on the way to helping yourself. In fact, the only truly prescriptive part of this book is advice offered so that you can help others cope with the new you.

If you have looked at the Table of Contents, you have noted that there are three parts to this book. The goal of Part I is to provide some insight into what it is you're doing, particularly to recognize in just how many little—and large—ways lies figure into your daily life. Undoubtedly you will recognize some people you know; hopefully you will learn something about yourself and how you relate to these people.

The next part provides a sometimes embarrassing, sometimes humorous look at hundreds of specific things we all say and do to convince others of our infallibility. Once you acknowledge that you tell these lies, they should seem funny—perhaps painfully so, because you'll be laughing at yourself. The goal here is to entertain while overcoming the resistance to acknowledging these lies. After acknowledging that you do tell lies, however, you can proceed to talk honestly about exactly what you do and whether you want to continue doing it.

This leads to the goal of Part III which is to seriously consider the consequences of all the time spent deceiving (or trying to, anyway) other people and yourself. While granting that we all are often, through societal structures and strictures, forced to deceive others, we must also acknowledge that all the deception creates a lot of pain for ourselves and others. Hopefully this will lead to an evaluation of the advantages and disadvantages of this deception and to a consideration of what situations and with what people you can stop the deceit.

Thus, rather than pointing an accusatory finger and indicting someone's character or mental stability, an attempt is made to analyze the benefits and costs of this behavior. Clearly, cutting back on the deceit must be recommended in some relationships. However, since it doesn't require great expertise or ingenious therapy to show how to stop lying, no attempt is made in this book to offer the pretense of a revolutionary cure. You stop lying by not telling lies—it's really as simple as that—and the only advice you may need concerns how to help other people cope with the resulting change in you. Therefore, the final chapter offers simple, constructive suggestions about how to work with friends to eliminate this barrier which—despite the possible contrary implication in the occasional attempts at levity—is a source of pain in our relationships and our lives.

*Jerald M. Jellison*

# I'M SORRY I DIDN'T MEAN TO

# AND OTHER **LIES** WE LOVE TO TELL

*1*

# WHY WE DO IT

# 1

# But I Really Am Sorry!

## *The Phenomenon of Lies, Justifications, Apologies, and Other Social Activities*

"I'm sorry the place is such a mess, but I have been so busy at work that there just hasn't been time to do a thing around the house."

"I apologize for being late, but the traffic was awful, and I had to search and search for a parking space."

"I hope instant coffee will be okay. My percolator isn't working, and besides, this instant is better than most."

3

"Well, these photos aren't as good as they could be because the lighting wasn't very good, and Susan kept jostling my elbow, and I think something was wrong with the film."

"I couldn't believe it—when I went to get dressed this morning everything I had to wear was at the cleaners, so I settled on these jeans."

"Gee, Mr. Jones, I'm sorry about the mistakes in the report, but I spent most of last night with a sick friend."

"I thought the movie was sensational! . . . Oh, well, I admit the story was a little trite, and you're right that Raquel Welch does seem an odd choice for *Little Women*. What I meant was that the camera work was really good, and didn't you think the editing was better than average?"

"Sorry, dear. I don't know what's wrong with me tonight. I've just had so much on my mind lately. Let's try again in the morning."

"I'm sorry. . ."

"I apologize. . ."

"I didn't mean to. . ."

And on and on it goes. Each of us has a repertoire of hundreds and hundreds of stock excuses and apologies and (like it or not) lies that we fall back on when the occasion calls for it. That doesn't mean, however, that we are "bad" because we sometimes don't tell the whole truth or even part of it. Nor should we feel guilt (that old "it's-a-sin-to-tell-a-lie" syndrome) because of it. We all do it, and we do it for good reasons—to be liked and to be accepted. It's a most important part of our behavior. And that is what this book is all about—our behavior, more particularly our inappropriate behavior. It's not so much about "why" we act inappropriately, but about what happens once we do. It's about our need to justify our actions and inactions to *other* people. It's about the lies we tell and the complications which result. It's about the tragic and funny things that we do. And it's about how we love doing it and hate doing it. And while we love other people, we hate them for making us do it. And it's about how we can break the habit—or at least reduce our dependence on it—make life easier and more enjoyable.

These excuses, explanations, and apologies are phenomena which I like to call "social justifications." They are *social*, rather than personal, because they are directed to other people rather than to ourselves. They are *justifications* because they are intended to prove that we are not as stupid, selfish, irresponsible, inconsiderate, cheap, or just plain inadequate as we might appear.

These omnipresent social justifications take a wide variety of forms. They can be non-verbal as well as verbal. For example, imagine walking down a street and thinking that you see an old acquaintance coming toward you. Just as your hand flashes into the air to wave, you realize it isn't your friend after all. Your hand, however, is in the middle of its action, so you subtly continue its movement upward in a slow, graceful arc and adjust a lock of hair. By adding these extra actions, you have transformed an inappropriate and presumptuous action into an innocuous sign of good grooming, thereby avoiding a stranger's suspicion and disapproval.

The goal of social justification is to put the blame for our mistakes on anything or anyone but ourselves. We blame the weather ("I just can't do a thing with my hair in this weather"), or the time of day ("I can't function until I've had a couple of cups of coffee in the morning"). We try to attribute our mistakes or shortcomings to our tools and equipment ("My tennis racket just isn't the same since it was restrung") or to our bodies ("I must have pulled something in my back the other day, because it really hurts when I serve"), but never to our character.

Social justifications can be as brief as a quick backward glance after tripping, which tells any observers that the real cause of our clumsiness was an object on the sidewalk. If we spill water from a glass or let a knife slip from our hand and clunk on the plate during dinner, we can just blurt out "oops" and keep right on eating and talking. During a serious post-dinner discussion, however, we might have to talk on for hours (in some cases, years) in order to socially justify why we haven't lived up to the promise of our youth or accomplished as much as an older sister, brother, or some other friendly rival.

We give social justifications for the things we didn't do as well as for the things we did ("I'm sorry I didn't come to see you before this. I really meant to, but I just didn't get a chance"). We socially justify things we did in the past ("I didn't send you a Christmas card this year because the increased cost of stamps forced us to cut back our list") or things we anticipate doing in the future ("I hope this won't offend you, but I just have to ask. . .").

We give social justifications throughout our lives. As children we quickly learned that it was much easier to get along with Mother if we said, "I'm sorry, I didn't mean to" after we knocked over one of her semiprecious knickknacks; or if we endearingly said, "But, Daddy told me it was okay" when we got caught sneaking a cookie. Our social justifications may become more subtle and sophisticated with age, but they don't decrease in frequency. As our bodies become less agile and our memories more fallible, we start acknowledging, "Well, I guess I'm not as young as I used to be."

Regardless of whether the social justification is expressed in words or by an action, or whether it is an excuse, an explanation, or an apology, it is basically a communication directed to other people. The primary message of all these communications is, "Don't blame me." Simply stated, social justifications are designed to convince the people around us that we aren't really as bad as our actions might imply.

We offer these apologies and excuses to avoid the anger and displeasure of others and to stave off the specter of social rejection and isolation. Hour by hour we engage in a continual process of giving socially acceptable reasons for our socially unacceptable behavior. We give explicit rationalizations to defend ourselves against the negative conclusions that we believe other people are drawing—always explaining because we are so often misunderstood.

Imagine that you followed someone throughout a complete day of activities, never actually observing him, but interviewing everyone with whom he came in contact. By early evening you might well conclude that you were on the trail of a saint. That is if he played the game well enough.

The individual you traced would have done many things which other people felt to be thoughtful, kind, sensible, or just plain nice. And after these good behaviors, the individual might have graciously accepted any proffered praise by saying, "It was nothing really," or "Oh, don't mention it." Those occasional inappropriate actions—inevitable on an average day—might well have vanished from the memory of those people you interviewed, erased or obscured by his program of apologies and excuses. What remained would be the sense of his "niceness." That is, of course, if everybody bought his act.

If, in fact, you went through a careful recounting of one person's morning and afternoon activities, what you might uncover would be many blundering actions that other people didn't judge to be either considerate or intelligent. But then, he never meant to do those bad things, did he? Every time he did something that caused pain or that wasn't quite right, he always had a good explanation. So, in a sense he didn't really do those bad things. Someone else or something else made him do them. *He* had only the best of intentions.

Few of us would be so naive as to accept this Pollyanna-like posturing. Yet we act as though *other* people *are* just that naive. In fact, we treat other people as though they're so naive that we can convince them that we virtually never make a mistake, and that we always act with the best of intentions and the loftiest ideals.

Even though we try to convince others that we are perfect, none of us is a saint and we know it. As if the hard, cold reality of both our behavior and our intentions were not bad enough, we then compound the impropriety by attributing our misdeeds to fictitious, or at least exaggerated, causes. The pattern is very simple and quickly becomes a routine—if we behave inappropriately, we check to see if anyone noticed; if anyone did, then we must give a social justification. Thus the cumulative effect of our justifications is a big lie—as far as our public persona is concerned, we are faultfree.

In addition to the big lie inherent in enacting the role of a saint, the specific justifications that we offer consist of a significant number of smaller lies. Sometimes the deceitful aspect of a social justification is very apparent; at other times getting beneath the veneer of honesty requires some analysis. Let's begin by examining the more transparent examples, starting with the "excuse."

> "Gee, Marie, I was looking forward to having dinner with you tonight, but my stomach has been bothering me all day, so I'd like to take a rain check."
> (Chances are he feels fine. He just found something else he'd rather do.)
> "Sorry, Hon, I'd love to talk longer, but I've got

to hang up. I've got something on the stove that's about to boil over." (Actually there is nothing on the stove, and Hon's friend certainly doesn't want to talk any longer.)

"I think we should end this relationship because I'm not good for you. It will be best for both of us this way." (You know the bastard secretly believes he's the best thing that ever happened in her life and that he's ending the relationship because it's in *his* best interest. The jerk.)

Next step up the ladder of social dishonesty is the "explanation." In defense of explanations, most people will say that they are simple and truthful (well, if not simple, at least truthful) descriptions of the facts surrounding our actions. But are they? Let's look closely at the purity of these "truthful explanations."

Most of us have had occasion to explain that we are late for an appointment because we couldn't find a parking space. This explanation probably was true and if challenged by the other party, we probably could have said with confidence, "Well if you don't believe me, just go and see for yourself." At first glance, it looks as though our integrity is vindicated, but there are other questions to answer. Would we have been late if it had been really important to be on time? Wouldn't we have taken every precaution and been on time to catch the plane that was to take us on the vacation we've been looking forward to for so long? Didn't we already know that parking is always a problem in that area and therefore shouldn't we have taken that into account and left home ten minutes earlier?

The point is, many of the factors which supposedly explain our errant behavior are factors that we actively chose not to avoid, thereby allowing them to affect our actions.

Further, if the actions had been truly important (i.e., strongly in our own self-interest), we would have made certain that we made no mistakes. So, we begin to see that even those "truthful explanations" contain a large measure of distortion and exaggeration of reality.

But then, what about apologies? Even if our excuses and explanations aren't completely honest, surely apologies are. Well, to the extent that we are expressing regret over a small, accidental thing, such as bumping into someone in an elevator or stepping on an inhabited shoe, we probably are sincerely "sorry." Of course, someone could argue that we could have been more careful, and true, we could have been. The point is that we didn't intend to bump into or step on someone and that we sincerely regret doing it. So these little apologies may be honest, but what about our big ones?

Probably the most familiar "I'm sorry, I didn't mean to. . ." occurs after particularly bitter arguments between lovers, spouses, or friends. Sometimes this type of major blowup results in an on-the-spot termination of the relationship. If it doesn't go quite that far, then the following scenario usually is acted out. Both parties are angry, and both to some extent have suffered a blow to the ego and/or bruised feelings. The less severely bruised, however, must make a conciliatory gesture, most commonly in the form of an apology (depending on the seriousness of the hurt, one may be allowed only a few seconds or as much as several days to make this apology). After the obligatory "I'm sorry," the remainder is usually something like, "I really didn't mean to say those things." Perhaps when we are in this kind of situation we do regret causing pain, but then what did we mean to do by lashing out at the other person in the first place?

If it had been the case that we didn't want to cause any pain at all, then we wouldn't have said anything even remotely cruel. Since we did say something vicious, it must have been the case that we did want to cause some hurt. Further, we were also aware that what we said probably wouldn't result in a complete termination of the relationship. If we expected that a temperamental outburst would cause our spouse to file for divorce, our lover to leave, our boss to fire us, a prized employee to quit, or some other equally disastrous and undesirable consequence, then we wouldn't have allowed ourselves to get so angry.

We may not have known exactly how much pain our statements would cause, but we did know there would be some. We could have predicted that our comments would not go unnoticed and unchallenged. At the same time, chances are we could have predicted that the consequences wouldn't be completely disastrous. We knew we would cause pain; that's what we intended, that's what we accomplished. Therefore, to say, "I'm sorry, I didn't mean to" has more than a hint of the lie to it.

So, whether we scrutinize excuses, explanations, or apologies, it is apparent that we are not telling the whole story when we socially justify. Further, by justifying we act as though we are perfect, incapable of error, and that too is patently not true. Given the everyday frequency with which we give social justifications, there can be no doubt that we love to do it. Anything we do that often has to provide some pleasure and satisfy some desire.

But in response to this assertion you might say, "Oh, *I* don't like to give social justifications. In fact, I hate it!" And when you're asked, "Well, why do you do it so often?" you would probably justify with, "Other people make me do it." Oh! It's not you. It's other people. You're an angel and those other people are devils. And it's probably also true that they've kidnapped you and are forcing you to stay in their company and treat them as friends.

Of course we like to justify! It's fun! We love to come up with a clever social justification which exonerates us from any blame. We feel proud of our quick-witted capacity to concoct an airtight defense which leaves other people speechless, and—on good days—regretting they ever challenged us. Frequently, in fact, when we do create an ingenious social justification which the other person accepts, we are encouraged to elaborate even further. Our thought seems to be, "Hmm-m-m. I got away with that one, so let me see what else I can get away with." These few joys associated with successfully justifying must, however, be balanced against the considerable pain we may also feel.

One of the pains connected with the addiction of justifying is that we are forced to be conscious of our every action. Even the most casual observation of everyday behavior reveals that most of us are constantly aware of the effect each of our actions is having on the people around us. We seem to operate on the assumption that others are scrutinizing our every action. We act as though the people who monitor our behavior not only watch what we do, but inquire of our every action, "Why did you do that?"

To assume that others are always implicitly questioning why we do everything is guaranteed to generate more than our daily recommended allowance of anxiety. But we get more, because that's not all we assume. We also think that the other person's answer to the question, "Why did you do that?" inevitably and invariably will be most unflattering to us. We act as though the unspoken answer to the unasked question, "Why is he late for our appointment?" will be "Because he's irresponsible." Similarly, "Why would she mispronounce that word?" will be answered with "She must not be very well educated." Or "Why did she go home and leave her desk in such a mess?" will bring the answer "She's just a sloppy and disorganized person."

And, if we politely tell the host at a party that we're enjoying ourselves, after having just described our utter boredom to a new acquaintance, then we panic for fear that our new friend will conclude that we are dishonest rather than that we expressed enjoyment out of consideration for the host's feelings. And of course, as writers such as Dear Abby remind us, when the ambulance delivers us to the emergency ward after the accident, all of the nurses and doctors will take one look at our less-than-sterile underclothes and conclude that we are one of the social untouchables.

Many of us act as though other people will make conclusive judgments about our total personality on the basis of one or two of our not-quite-appropriate actions. We seem to fear that one dumb comment will be interpreted as evidence that we are total idiots, that a single statement of self-praise will be treated as an indication that we are egotistical braggards, or that saying anything at all negative about females will be interpreted to mean that we oppose equality for women.

Fearing that others will draw these over-generalized conclusions about our character, we feel compelled to do something so that their answer to "Why did you do that?" will not go unchallenged. We feel we must say something in our own defense, so the flood of excuses, explanations, and apologies to try to avert total social disgrace.

The most immediate consequences of offering a social justification is the pleasure of avoiding the pain of being disliked and rejected. If we didn't justify, there might well be a disturbing and painful argument involving unpleasant accusations, recriminations, and hurt feelings. This short-run pleasure has narcotic effects and reinforces the pattern of giving justifications which in the long run can have some very unpleasant and lasting effects. As already noted, one of the undesirable consequences of habitual justifying is that it is only a matter of time before we move from relatively true and factual explanations to outright lies.

In order to be prepared to give our little lie, we must constantly be on guard to determine whether we've committed some error that should be quickly justified. Most of us have had the experience of blithely driving along in our car when suddenly we notice a police car behind us. There is no indication that the officer wants us to pull over or that he is after us. Even so, we are overwhelmed with anxiety as we get the idea that he is going to give us a ticket. We begin to think that the police officer is scrutinizing our every move and that he is searching for some reason, no matter how insignificant, to give us a ticket. And, in fact, the combination of the anxiety and the self-consciousness might even cause us to commit some mistake that warrants a ticket. (Of course, the officer is unlikely to accept the justification that he caused us to break the law and would still give us the dreaded ticket.)

The armed forces used to advertise: "The price of security is constant defense." For most people the price of "social security" is paid in unremitting anxiety, apprehension, and mental torment. In order to be prepared to justify we must always worry about whether others think we are doing "okay." This fear of being watched generates a small dose of paranoia which we have come to take as almost normal or expected, just a part of life. It is only when we experience the relief of being completely accepted by someone (or when we're alone) that we fully realize the burden of this paranoia.

Closely associated with our paranoia of surveillance by others are deeply felt but seldom expressed feelings of anger and resentment. For example, we would be angry that the police officer appeared behind us and we would resent him having the right to decide whether or not we should be punished. Although we seldom overtly express our anger and resentment at the constant surveillance and punitiveness of others, we all sense it's there. Those feelings of joy and exaltation when we snub our noses at social convention, or tell a petty rule-enforcer where to get off, result from months and years of frustration and suppressed anger. We can't overtly express our anger (that would be inappropriate and would just require more justification), but we can enjoy the freedom of heroes such as R. P. McMurphy in *One Flew Over the Cuckoo's Nest,* living without apparent regard for the rules of others.

The anxiety, the paranoia about others' negative judgments, the self-consciousness, and the lying, all contribute to and feed on our feelings of self-doubt. Our fear that others think we are flawed gives rise to that same feeling within ourselves. When we lie in order to get out of some unpleasant situation, we privately recognize our dishonesty and record it as just another one of our faults. In part our anxiety stems from doubts about our own ability to behave the way we should, but that very anxiety causes us to commit errors which become the basis for even more self-doubt. And so a vicious cycle of worry and concern about our own value as individuals becomes another part of the social justification habit.

With all these negative consequences, it's only natural to wonder how people get caught in this mess in the first place. Why do we keep doing it? And is there any way out? Is it possible to extricate ourselves, to kick the habit? How can we go about it? To answer questions such as these, it will be necessary to more fully explore the phenomenon of social justification. We need to know some of the subtle details of the process involved every time we decide to give a justification. We need to know all of the complicated and ingenious methods we employ in our effort to socially justify our behavior.

# 2

# Pardon Me While I Straighten My Halo

*The Standards by which
We (Pretend to) Live*

For better *and* worse, human social groups are characterized by an unending supply of unwritten rules governing—even dictating—our social interactions. These rules, or standards of behavior, indicate the way people should and shouldn't behave. They become the social norms and form the basis of our expectations about the way "nice" people do things. Nice people keep their promises; nice people keep their homes, offices, children, cars, and themselves neat and clean; they act rationally, and say intelligent things. Nice

17

people *don't* make early morning phone calls, monopolize conversations, serve cheap food or liquor, publicly stick their fingers in their mouth, nose, or ears, nor do other socially unattractive things.

The scope of these standards for behavior ranges from the subtle aspects of specific actions to extended series of behaviors. We concern ourselves not only with a person's general lifestyle, but also with the precise way he smiles. We make sweeping judgments concerning a person's job or lack thereof ("Never will make anything of himself"), living arrangements ("Why they're not even married!), basic competencies ("Can't drive a car. . .pound a nail. . .spell cat. . .boil water. . .feed himself"), and primary motives ("Oh, she's only interested in what's in it for her"). At the more specific level we are concerned with the nature of a handshake (ugh, too limp; oooh, too firm), the use of silverware (is it the fat fork with three prongs, or the skinny one with two?), and the way words are pronounced (theater, vase, warsh).

The number and variety of these standards is truly astounding. They extend from the most mundane and routine individual actions, such as personal hygiene, to the sublime, such. as a person's manner of expressing affection. Some standards are applicable to our jobs, others to our play and recreation. There are sets of standards for acquiring and consuming material goods and thousands more for conducting interpersonal matters. We have elaborate rules concerning the preparation, serving, and consumption of food and drinks, even more complex and potentially treacherous ones for making love.

There is no sphere of human activity that is not covered by rules and, as a result, standardized. And, of course, the number of these standards is constantly increasing. As soon as some new machine (pocket calculators), implement (credit cards), type of food (frozen yogurt), or activity (personal and minority group liberation) is introduced into a social setting, new standards for behavior are developed. For example, when marijuana became popular, a set of rules quickly evolved to specify the right way to roll a joint, hold your breath, and handle a roach. To not do these things correctly is, in those circles, to not be with it. Occasionally specific standards disappear, as when a fad in clothing or dancing changes, but just as one fad replaces another, so too does one standard replace another.

Now obviously the purpose of these standards for behavior is to get people to act in particular ways. But human beings have an occasional tendency not to behave in these particular ways, even though they fully know they're supposed to. This tendency has been dutifully recognized and in turn is covered by a subsidiary set of rules. For example, marital fidelity is prescribed, but if someone decides to have an affair, then there are standards specifying the right ways and the wrong ways to do it. Similarly, you shouldn't lie or engage in deception, but if you must, then you should do it with a certain care, concern, and finesse. Both formal laws and informal standards prohibit theft and graft, but these things do go on and so there are even standards covering how to steal from an employer, how to accept a bribe, and how to cheat on an income tax return.

The process of learning these standards for behavior begins almost at birth, and as we increase in age, so do the rules we're supposed to know and abide by. Each major transition in life involves acquiring another set of standards. Moving from high school to college, from college to a job, or moving from one neighborhood to another, from one part of the country to another, or starting a marriage or family—all require learning and living by more and different standards. The increased mobility and rapidly changing technology of contemporary life puts great pressure on us to continually integrate new standards of behavior. In fact, one of the characteristics associated with the successful people in contemporary society is the ability to incorporate new standards and to alter their behavior appropriately, quickly, and effortlessly.

These unwritten standards for behavior are so complex and so numerous that they are sometimes contradictory. For example, we are supposed to be generous and help others, *and* we are also admonished to take care of old number one. We're supposed to be trusting *and* suspicious. We're supposed to take certain risks, *and* also to be cautious. The balancing of these apparently conflicting demands quickly produces frustration, grey hair, and fantasies of escaping to a deserted island.

Some of the general conflicts which exist between standards are aggravated because the standards applicable to one situation are not exactly the same as those relevant to another situation. We are required to act one way at home, another way at the office, and yet another way in more public places. The relevant standards also depend upon exactly who is sharing the situation with us. Our relations with strangers are governed by different standards than those applied to close friends, which are different from the standards applied to relatives, or to a spouse, or children, or an employer, or, or, or. We are expected to adapt to each subtle difference in each situation. . .or else!

Further complicating the process of our general adjustment is the fact that standards for behavior specify not only *what* behavior is appropriate but also exactly *how, when, where, with whom,* and *how much* to engage in that behavior. To appreciate the detailed filigree of these standards, let's look at a few examples.

Nothing could be more basic than the consumption of

food. Human beings, however, with their clever use of rules and standards, have managed to transform the simple act of eating into a complex task which exceeds the capacity of all children and most adults. The rules about *how* to eat are so complex that they require two chapters in a book of etiquette (the gist of which is to act as though you're not really hungry). The usual answer to the question of *when* to eat is three times a day, with mid-morning, afternoon, and late night snacks also permitted. Eating more frequently than this (six times sounds like plenty), however, is inappropriate, especially immediately after a meal. As we all also know, there are only certain places where it is all right to eat. Around the home, eating in the kitchen and dining room is fine, but eating in the living room, bedroom, and bathroom—especially the bathroom—is not so good. For eating outside the home, there are designated areas, usually with tables or counters, in which you won't bother other people and they won't bother you (too much). But, you shouldn't eat while walking down the street, while standing in line to pay at a cafeteria, or while seated on the ground unless there is a blanket of some kind and we label it a "picnic." We don't seem to worry very much about *with whom* to eat. Friends are better than strangers, but that isn't crucial. The only crucial rule seems to be that the other person have as much food and no greater an appetite. (No one wants to eat while someone else is drooling nearby.) The final issue of *how much* is clearly covered by rules and can be the subject of considerable controversy best left to Dr. Atkins and the other diet experts. Let's say simply that it is possible to eat too much and too little.

As another example of the many things that are specified by standards, consider the behavior of talking about personal matters. We should only talk about such things with people who really care, (i.e., spouse, parents, close friends) or with people who don't care at all (strangers on planes, trains, or buses), but people whose caring is in between these two extremes (the guy at the next desk, someone you've only dated once or twice, your boss) are out. Such talk should be conducted behind closed doors or in the wide open spaces and one's tone should always be serious and somewhat dramatic. On the question of *how often,* we find again that a moderate amount is best. To never discuss one's personal concerns is considered a sign of excessive secretiveness and is regarded with suspicion; to discuss such matters frequently is considered a sign of neuroticism and is regarded as boring by most everyone but therapists. Small children frequently cause their parents a great deal of embarrassment because they discuss the family's personal affairs in the wrong places and with the wrong people.

In general, it is probably the case that the more personal or important a behavior is judged to be, the greater will be the details prescribed by the standards. For example, the rules dealing with sexual behavior cover all of the factors itemized above. Everyone knows the rules about with whom (never with a stranger), where (definitely an indoor activity), when (not during working hours), and how often (neither a satyr nor a celibate be). Recently the matter of exactly how has become a matter of considerable discussion, as more publications recommend and seemingly condone a greater variety of acts and techniques. This controversy need not concern us, since our goal is not to pass judgment on these standards but instead simply to recognize their existence and become aware of their detail and specificity.

Given the infinite number, variety, and complexity of these standards for behavior, it is hardly surprising that we often fail to live up to all of them. The larger the number of standards for behavior to which we subscribe, the more likely it is that we will inevitably violate them. All of us at some point will say the "wrong" thing at the "wrong" time. We fail to keep all of our promises. We behave improperly. We occasionally display a lack of or lapses in intelligence, taste, honesty, responsibility, and concern-for-others. We frequently allow ourselves to show too much interest in the "wrong" people (the opposite sex, degenerates, ourselves) and the "wrong" things (television, football, gossip), and too little interest in those people (loved ones, superiors) and things (taking out the garbage, keeping within the budget) to which we should attend.

While it is easy to see how we manage to get into so much trouble, what with the complexity of rules and so forth, it is much more difficult to pinpoint and comprehend the method by which others decide we're in trouble. The basics of the process involve simply taking a behavior that someone performed and comparing it to a standard. By virtue of this comparison process, a behavior is judged to be congruent with the standard or it is judged to be incongruent with the standard, in other words, okay or not okay. The comparison process itself, therefore, results in a simple, dichotomous decision: a behavior is either appropriate or inappropriate. But is it so simple?

Being in the presence of someone who is either very self-righteous or filled with contempt for you personally provides ample evidence of the speed with which people can make judgments about the appropriateness of behavior. This speed, however, belies the subtlety of the process. Let's look at this process a little more closely by asking, "What is a behavior?" A definition of what is meant by a behavior may seem unnecessary since it obviously involves the kinds of things we all do all the time—talking, eating, working, grooming, etc. Don't be fooled: as we will see later, a whole realm of social justifications is based on the issue of exactly what behavior did or did not occur. In discussing social justification, therefore, it becomes crucial to understand when one specific behavior begins and ends, and when another one commences. For example, if Joe makes a comment and Bill butts in, saying, "That's ridiculous," Joe may well respond, "Please, I haven't finished what I was saying!" Or, if the host is in the midst of making his favorite papaya/cranberry punch and a guest scoops out a quick glassful and exclaims, "Eccch! That tastes terrible!" the host may respond indignantly, "I'm not finished yet!" Both Joe and the host are indicating that their *behavior* is not yet completed. In both cases the actual behavior unit is longer than what Bill and the guest have perceived.

For our present purposes we will consider a *behavior* as an integrated sequence of acts. The beginning and end of the sequence that makes up the behavior are defined by the goal toward which the action is directed (e.g., making a point in conversation, baking a cake, ordering a drink, lighting a cigarette, or making love). Once the goal of one sequence is reached, that behavior is finished and another sequence of actions will be initiated.

Since some goals can be achieved very quickly and simply (winking your eye to indicate a desire for friendship or a desire to pay a certain price at an auction), some behaviors may consist of only one or two acts. Other goals are more difficult to achieve and the behavior will consist of a complicated and extended sequence of actions. For example, imagine a novice in an expensive French restaurant about to engage in the act of ordering a meal. The first step in the sequence involves getting the attention of the professionally aloof waiter. Next he orders the main dish (in French or with pointed finger), then the vegetables, the salad, the salad dressing, the wine (what type? what vintage? how expensive?), and finally requests that coffee be served at the end of the meal. As any anxious newcomer to this situation can testify, it is possible to demonstrate a blatant lack of sophistication, confidence, wealth, and/or savoir-faire by blundering on any of the sub-acts included in the whole behavioral sequence. Once the goal of ordering the meal is achieved, our neophyte might engage in the act of lighting a cigarette. This behavior is briefer, but it also consists of a sequence of sub-acts: removing the cigarette pack and matches from the pocket; nonchalantly extracting one cigarette (sometimes no small task); inserting the cigarette in your mouth (the filter end goes where?); striking *one* match; lighting the *end* of the cigarette; taking one big puff; extinguishing the match; exhaling while not coughing; returning matches and pack to pocket without reading the Surgeon General's warning.

Now, keeping in mind this understanding of what is meant by a behavior, we can return to the initial question, exactly how *do* people make a decision about the appropriateness of a behavior, or conversely, what makes our actions inappropriate? It is apparent that since a behavior is a sequence of sub-acts, we can err by not properly executing the sequence. Thus, we might *delete* one or more of the sub-acts in the sequence, like forgetting to put out the match. Or, we might do all of the prescribed sub-acts but somehow *misorder* them (putting the matches back in your pocket without ever lighting the cigarette). Or, we might do everything, and in the right order, but our error might be in *adding* some unnecessary acts to the sequence (immediately lighting a second cigarette). The way in which these three criteria (deletion, misordering, addition) operate can likewise be illustrated by returning to our neophyte in the French restaurant. Since the behavior involved in this instance is quite complex and subtle, there is even more room for error. Our neophyte could bungle the behavior of ordering the meal by deleting one of the acts in the sequence, such as not ordering the vegetables. He could misorder the acts by requesting Roquefort dressing before specifying the type of salad. (Of course, we've all had the experience of being with someone who misorders the sequence by beginning with the dessert selection. As they say in French restaurants, "Quelle faux pas!") Finally, our neophyte might have performed the behavior of ordering the dinners admirably and then gauche it up by adding, "Oh, yes, and bring us the mint-flavored toothpicks when you serve the coffee."

Perhaps it should be pointed out that deletion can range from not performing one or two of the sub-acts in a sequence to the extreme form of deleting all of them. Thus, it may be that we are supposed to do something (make dinner reservations, pick up milk and bread at the store, formally introduce our new friend to our old acquaintances at a party), but fail to do any part of it.

In addition to judging behaviors as inappropriate because we didn't perform them in the traditionally proper sequence, people also use some less precise criteria for dealing with the quality of our actions. One such qualitative factor is the intensity or enthusiasm with which we act. For example, the act of shaking hands may be deemed inappropriate because it is done with either too little intensity (limp fish) or too great an intensity (bone crusher). More generally, it is possible to express too much enthusiasm about some things (the attractiveness of someone else's husband or wife) and too little about others (the attractiveness of your own mate). Almost any action can be judged as inappropriate because it didn't have the proper degree of intensity or enthusiasm. In fact, if people can't legitimately criticize you for what you did, they frequently resort to attacking the intensity with which you did it.

This dimension of intensity can be used as a weapon in interpersonal relations. Disgruntled children are quick to learn that they can really irritate their parents and thereby get some revenge by performing required behaviors with an inappropriate degree of intensity. This typically occurs when the parent is standing nearby to make certain that the child does what was requested. For example, children very cleverly brush their teeth with either too much enthusiasm or too little. Similarly, they'll wash their hands with the intensity of someone who just touched poison, or with so little intensity that they are bound to get you angry. When you do complain, they offer the lament, "But I *am* doing it."

Adults also use intensity as a weapon. We all find ourselves, against our wishes, in situations where we are doing something solely to please someone else. We, too, protest this supposedly cruel and inhuman treatment by acting with too much or too little attention. When forced to attend a stuffy concert, we might act overly enthusiastic by ostentatiously cocking our head and sitting on the edge of the seat, or we might close our eyes and yawn to demonstrate our marked lack of interest. When forced to go shopping at a sleazy discount store, we might show our disdain by acting completely uninterested in the merchandise or by exclaiming the virtues and beauty of each plastic novelty or wash-and-wear outfit. When our lover's desire for sex is as positive as our attitude is negative, we might protest being forced into the act by reacting with as little enthusiasm as is possible.

Closely related to the qualitative dimension of intensity is the time factor—how long we take to execute a behavioral sequence. Here again, moderation is the rule, with both too much time and too little time generally deemed inappropriate. When someone keeps her eyes focused on another person for too long, we accuse her of staring; when an employee spends too much time at the water fountain, we accuse him of goofing off; and when we leave the steaks on the grill too long, we are accused of being absentminded and/or stupid. Conversely, we may sometimes speak too fast, gulp our food, or hurry with sex.

In sum, the exact process by which people decide that a behavior is inappropriate or appropriate entails a detailed analysis of the sequence of acts performed, plus the intensity and amount of time associated with them. Regardless of how complicated the process may be, there is no doubt that human beings are all Olympic gold medalists at making such judgments. People can make them very quickly and can do it day after day with unlimited endurance.

Now that the details of the process of comparing behavior to standards have been outlined, we can turn to the consequences of this comparison process. In this regard, our major concern will be the kinds of judgments people make about us, based on our behavior, and how we, in turn, interpret and react to those judgments.

# 3

# I Just Want
# to Be Loved

*Lying and the Fight
for Survival*

When people compare our behavior to a standard and decide that we behaved appropriately, they immediately—and probably without being aware of it—assume that we did it simply because it is "the proper thing to do." But when the judgment is that we behaved inappropriately, the answer to the "why" question is invariably that we possess undesirable personal qualities (i.e., there is something "wrong" with us).

This process of making a judgment or inference about

an individual's personal characteristics based on his behavior is known as "attribution." Logically enough, this process involves attributing the cause of an individual's behavior to his needs, motives, values, attitudes, or abilities. For example, if someone tries to boss everyone around, we might attribute this behavior to an excessive power motivation or to insecurity (i.e., need for attention and love). If we catch someone in a lie, we question her values and assume that she doesn't value honesty. If an employee is late for work all the time and only puts out a half-hearted effort when there, we might attribute this behavior to a "bad attitude." Likewise, when someone fails in doing something that requires a certain degree of talent or ability, we deem him inept or incompetent.

But what if you were told you were going to meet a person you're sure to like, but whose most outstanding traits are dishonesty, stupidity, selfishness, laziness, and crudeness? "He must have some good traits," you say. "No. Just bad ones." Couldn't you like him anyway? What? You only like people with good qualities! Hmm? It seems that you're like most people then. All of us like "nice" people, those with good characteristics, and dislike those with bad traits or qualities. The point is that the practical consequence of attributing an undesirable quality to someone is that we disapprove of or dislike that person.

Of course, as in all things subjective, there are gradations to these "likes" and "dislikes." If we don't know the person who behaves inappropriately, our "liking" of him is reduced from zero to "disliking." If we already dislike the person, then his inappropriate action will make our reaction even more negative—say, something on the verge of "despise." If someone we initially like behaves inappropriately, our liking for that person may be only slightly reduced. If the person is already our friend, he has a good form of in-

surance, because when he does something "wrong" the
amount of disfavor he incurs won't be as great as if he had
committed the same blunder in front of someone who didn't
know him or like him. The fact that people are less harsh on
people they like than on people they dislike should not,
however, obscure the basic fact that an inappropriate behavior will reduce, to some degree, people's affection for an
individual, regardless of how much they may like him initially.

With people we dislike, we immediately translate our
reaction to their inappropriate behavior into a further reduction of our already almost non-existent liking for them. ("I
loathe *and* despise him!") On the other hand, with people
we like, we may not immediately decrease our liking after
each of their inappropriate behaviors. ("Aw, well, you
know Charlie.") Even though we don't reduce our liking for
them, we record the instance of inappropriate behavior and
if they repeat it once or twice again, we might dramatically
and quite unexpectedly decrease our liking for them. ("That
does it, Charlie. You'll hear from my lawyer.") Regardless
of whether the translation from inappropriate behavior to de-
creased liking and disapproval is immediate or delayed, the
basic point, which we all implicitly understand, is that every
significant inappropriate behavior has the very real potential
of making other people like us less.

And this brings us to one of life's major inequities. Although behaving inappropriately inevitably results in exile,
alienation, thoughts of suicide, or at least a social snub, behaving appropriately does not make us heroes or even the
most popular in our class. Appropriate behavior is *expected*,
and by behaving appropriately we simply hold our own as
average human beings (whatever *they* are). Behaving appropriately implies only that we are normal—not that we are
special or that we are worthy of attention and love. *That*

you have to work for. You must do something that most people wouldn't do (like babysit with your boss's chihuahua) or that is extraordinary in some way (*asking* to do it a second time!). For example, most employees won't work past quitting time unless they are paid for it, but you could win approval if you not only worked overtime without thought of compensation, but if you did it on your birthday, even though you had carefully announced to everyone that you had a big evening planned. Many people will call or visit when you are sick with some minor thing, but how many people will visit once a day and call twice a day or bring you soup and juice even though your flu is highly contagious? And, as "B" movies have made famous, when attempting to guarantee a comfortable place close to dowdy old Aunt Mildred's heart and near the top of her will, we'll endure seemingly endless afternoon teas and monologues about "the good old days."

Aside from these special occasions when we go out of our way to demonstrate our outstanding personal characteristics, the general result of appropriate behavior is that we maintain the minimal impression of acceptability ("he's okay, but nothing special"). Once we realize and accept the fact that appropriate behavior doesn't earn us any medals, make us stars, or even insure popularity but merely defends us from possible social rejection, one of the unpleasant truths of contemporary life becomes distressingly clear: In most of our interpersonal relationships we walk a narrow tightrope above an abyss of social disgrace, disapproval, personal failure, loneliness, and pain. An inappropriate behavior represents the one false step that may cause us to fall from grace. Being a regular person and doing all the appropriate things doesn't widen the rope or put a net under us; rather it allows us to continue walking on the tightrope.

It is clear, therefore, why we do engage in social justification, even if it means lying. We *must* make other people like us; we can't risk social rejection, even if the penalty is not liking ourselves. And so we justify our actions, to eliminate the taint of undesirability, to alter a negative impression, and just to maintain our status of being "normal."

Although most of us keep our eyes wide open for those subtle signs of disapproval expressed on the faces of other people, such vigilance is not always necessary. An occasional person, one revered and feared for her bluntness, will say something like, "Why did you do a dumb thing like that?" or "I had no idea just how selfish you are." Mercifully, such traumatizingly explicit statements of disapproval are rare and usually come only from very close friends or very close enemies. More likely than not, people will inwardly record their negative judgments, but—unless caught off guard—will allow only minimal acknowledgement of their immediate reaction to our mistake. True, they may later talk openly about it behind our backs, but in our presence its only manifestation may be a subtle change in facial expression or posture. It is for this reason that we are ever alert, always reading the hidden meaning in those raised eyebrows, drooping smiles, or eyes which look at us a little too long or reflect an expression of shock.

In determining the magnitude of the disapproval directed toward us, we take our cues primarily from the other person's immediate verbal statements or nonverbal signals of disapproval. However, prior knowledge of a standard's importance to a person is also a consideration. If we have observed our boss blow up when a fellow employee forgot to lock up at night, then we quiver as we approach the office the morning after we too failed to lock the safe or doors. Or, if a friend has previously told us how much importance she attaches to a particular standard, then we may infer that her immediate controlled reaction to our breaking that standard does not necessarily represent the full extent of her anger and disapproval. Parents sometimes conceal the full extent of their disapproval of a child's bad behavior because of the presence of other people. The child knows from past experience, however, that rage lurks behind the parent's calm facial exterior, and he dreads seeing the other people leave.

There is danger, however, in anticipating disapproval. We sometimes socially justify our actions before we've had a chance to observe just how much disapproval we have actually generated. This is usually the case when we are quite aware of the importance an observer attaches to a standard we have just violated. If we swear in front of a very formal person, we will immediately apologize and explain the source of frustration or injustice that caused our obscene outburst. ("I can't believe I said that! I'm sorry, I'm just under so much pressure.") Sometimes, however, we are better off pretending that nothing happened. Social justification in the absence of any overt sign of disapproval from the observer can often lead to unintended and undesirable consequences. For example, take the man who leaves the office early in order to have a brief visit with his mistress, and who then arrives home some 5 to 10 minutes later than usual. No sooner is he in the door than he is offering excuses for being late (his boss, the traffic, flat tire, etc.). His wife, who hadn't even noticed and who hadn't given the slight delay a second thought, may infer from these enthusiastic excuses that something is amiss ("Has my husband been engaged in inappropriate behavior?"). Thus suspicion is generated about the actual reason for the husband's lateness. He had anticipated disapproval where none actually existed, with the result that his justifications caused suspicion that something heinous had taken place. His big miscalculation was that his immediate behavior—being 5 to 10 minutes late—was not so inappropriate or unusual as to necessitate such extensive justification.

Justifications in response to anticipated, rather than indicated, social disapproval are most apt to occur in situations where the nature and importance of the other person's standards are well-defined and we have had some experiences against which we can estimate the other's judgment of our behavior. The fact that we sometimes engage in social justification before anyone has indicated disapproval does not contradict the assertion that the justification is social (for the benefit of the other person) rather than personal (for the sake of our own conscience or ego). In the previous example, the man was reacting to anticipated disapproval. There is no doubt that the expectation of anger and disapproval from others can be as real and have as much effect on us as their actual reaction.

Regardless of whether other people translate their attribution of an undesirable trait into actual disliking for us, and regardless of whether this disapproval is expressed overtly, subtly, or is simply anticipated, our social justifications are designed to cope with *their* negative reactions, not our own. Again, these are *social* justifications designed to improve our public's perception of our worth, not *personal* justifications meant to satisfy our private, subjective self-evaluations.

That social justifications are aimed solely at counteracting the negative impressions of others can be demonstrated in several ways. First, many of our justifications range from outright lies to serious distortions of reality; we know they are false when we give them. And although we act (often convincingly) as if they were true, we'll never really come to believe them. Examples range from the trivial to the serious. The man who tilts his head to gaze at a woman's legs, and then when caught pretends to be stretching his neck, is never himself going to believe he actually had a neck cramp. Likewise the alcoholic who creates the myth of a chronically sick mother in an effort to justify her frequent absences from work—she may live with the lie for years, but she knows it will never be true. According to traditional analytic theory, we must actually believe the personal rationalizations we use in justifying our actions to ourselves. ("People are hostile to me because I am attractive, and they are jealous.") Supposedly these personal defense mechanisms only work if we actually believe them. In contrast, the success of social justification depends on the other person believing it.

Second, if these justifications were meant to placate our own internal demons of doubt, then why would we say them out loud? Why announce these things to others if we're only trying to convince ourselves? Further, if these justifications were designed to raise our self-esteem, then we would proffer them after any inappropriate behavior regardless of who saw the misdeed. But we don't. We give social justifications only if we think someone else saw the action *and* judged it to be inappropriate. Additionally, as we will explore in a later section, we only justify to someone when we want and need his or her approval. We don't as a rule justify to people who don't have as much power as we do (busboys, hotel maids, custodians, children) unless they have something we need at that particular time, or if what we did was so grossly inappropriate that their knowledge of it gives them potential (blackmail) power over us. If we blunder in someone's presence and can't come up with a good justification at the time, we'll keep thinking about it until we invent one, and then offer it the very next time we see that person.

A third demonstration of the fact that this is a social phenomenon is that we offer justifications even though we don't personally view our behavior as inappropriate. It is enough merely that someone else views it that way—someone we consider important. We have all gone through the chores of cleaning up the house or apartment simply because someone who might disapprove of our sloppiness was coming over. If that someone dropped in unexpectedly, we would justify profusely for the condition of the place simply because we value the other person's opinion of us, or because we know that that person believes neatness and order to be important. Most of us don't personally believe that our living quarters have to look like something from *House Beautiful,* and therefore don't justify to friends who share our beliefs.

There are times, of course, when we too know that we have behaved inappropriately. But shame and guilt need not necessarily be present—we would justify anyway. Conversely, we may judge one of our behaviors to be inappropriate, but as long as the other person hasn't noticed or doesn't seem to think it was so bad, we'll let it go. Why publicly acknowledge our error by justifying?

In sum, social justifications are quite different from what Freudian theory labels defense mechanisms. Supposedly we use defense mechanisms to justify our behavior to our own conscience or superego. It may not be unreasonable to assert that these rationalizations that we play with in our minds represent nothing more than the mental testing or rehearsal of possible justifications we can later give to others. That is, what has traditionally been viewed as an internal process of the ego may simply be the preparatory stage for future public actions or statements.

In comparison to traditional analyses of human affairs, it is accurate to say that we give social justifications in order to avoid the disapproval of someone else, rather than to assuage any internal personal disapproval. Strictly speaking, however, to explain social justification in terms of a desire to avoid social disapproval doesn't tell the whole story. To pursue this explanation a little further we could ask, "Why do we want to avoid the disapproval?" Many people would subscribe to answers such as: "Everyone knows that we need the approval and respect of others," or "To assuage the hurt, avoid the loneliness, fill the void, boost the ego, and generally 'be there' and show acceptance." Perhaps these explanations are adequate for some purposes, but it is possible to develop a different response to the question.

Let's consider the advantages of being liked by others rather than being disliked by them. When someone disapproves of us, he usually will ignore us, offering us nothing but a cold shoulder and a deaf ear. However, if he actively dislikes us, it means that he won't want to be around us, won't offer us help, and in fact may even harm us. Someone who dislikes us won't invite us to parties, won't prepare dinner for us, help us to move our furnishings, give us a ride, loan us money, or invite us to spend the night. Engendering someone's disfavor may cause him to insult or embarrass us in public, "stab us in the back," kick us out of the house, and possibly even abuse us physically! Now, isn't it nicer to be liked?

If disapproval means social ostracism or, worse yet, physical pain, it is easy to understand why we want to avoid or reduce the disapproval created by our inappropriate behavior. We want to avoid disapproval, because if we don't we'll reap consequences that may make life very difficult and unpleasant. In other words, it is not the statements of disapproval that scare us, but the potential consequences of that disapproval.

This reasoning suggests that, conversely, people who like us should do nice things for us. Of course, it doesn't always seem to work out that way. Many of us can cite instances in which people who supposedly liked us, or even said they loved us, caused considerable pain. But note, the reference is to people who *supposedly* like us; here we are dealing with people who *actually* like us. Further, the fact that someone does like us doesn't (as they will often tell us) necessarily imply that he or she doesn't like someone or something else more, and, although they love us, this does not mean that all their actions will reflect this love. Also, it is clear that the people we let love us have the greatest potential to cause us pain. But that isn't quite the point here either. We're not concerned with potentials or occasional instances. We're concerned with whether, in general, people who actually like us do things which are to our benefit and attempt to protect us from harm.

If you need a job, you ask your friends if they know of one. When you need a quick, uncomplicated loan, you seek out the people who like you. A remark such as, "If you're ever in our part of the country (or our country), you know that you have a place to eat and sleep" usually is made (and meant) only by people who like us. Similarly, we feel most comfortable in asking people who know and like us to get things for us wholesale, to get us good tickets for a show or concert, to give an honest appraisal of a used car, to provide inside information on something important to us, to protect us from mental and physical bullies, and to care for us when we're sick and love us when we're well. In other words, it is the people who like us who are more apt to give us the things we need to sustain us and to allow us to enjoy life. The implication in terms of the present analysis is that we want and need the approval of others so that we can get these very real benefits. It is the material consequences of social approval (or disapproval) rather than the other person's opinion in and of itself that causes us to seek approval.

Perhaps a hypothetical example will best serve to illustrate this. Imagine applying for a job and going through the
rigors of a series of tests, until you are one of three people
selected for a final interview with the head of personnel.
Since your qualifications are basically the same as those of
your two competitors, you know you really have to make an
impression in the interview if you are to get the job. (And
you really want that job, because the money will enable you
to begin eating again, to move out of your crummy
neighborhood, and to buy a Mexican velvet painting.) But
what kind of impression are you going to create? You want
to create a positive impression, of course, and get the personnel manager to like and approve of you. Just before the
interview, however, as you're waiting to be called into the
personnel manager's office, you overhear her laughing as
she talks on the phone to the president of the company.
She's laughing as she explains how she has learned that the
job applicants she personally likes and enjoys never work
out well upstairs in the production offices. You hear this
and blink in disbelief as she confidentially explains to the
caller that for this job, unlike the ones before it, she'll hire
the individual she personally dislikes.

Now what are you going to do? If you believe what
you have just overheard, and there is every reason that you
should, then you will try to get the personnel manager to
dislike you. She calls you in: She comments on the beautiful
day. You say, "Ecch, who needs it?" While walking into
her office you notice her signature on the watercolors on the
wall. Your response is: "Is your daughter in kindergarten?
She'll never be a Grandma Moses, but then it's easy for
parents to ignore a lack of talent." When you notice the
look of shock and disapproval on her face, you don't bother
to socially justify. You know you're really rolling now;
surely the job is yours!

This example may seem unrealistic, but when people were confronted with a comparable situation in a laboratory experiment, they did everything they could to create a negative impression. Our purpose, however, is to illustrate the idea that it is not the approval or disapproval per se that we react to but the rewards or punishments which are usually directly related to approval and disapproval. Thus, in the example when the job (a very big reward) was made contingent upon disapproval, we would expect the individual to seek disapproval. It is the material consequences that we are really concerned about and only secondarily the other person's approval. Of course, the usual case is that we get rewards from people who like us, so we try to get and use their approval, and attempt to avoid their disapproval.

To sum up, let's look again at the issue that initiated this extended analysis: "Why do we justify?" The obvious answer was, "We do it in order to avoid the disapproval of others," which answer in turn led to the question, "Why do we attempt to avoid disapproval?" We saw that for some purposes it might be sufficient to simply assume that human beings have a need for the approval of others and by implication a need to avoid disapproval. In contrast to this perspective, the analysis just presented suggests that we attempt to seek approval and avoid disapproval simply because of the material consequences that are contingent upon another's opinion of us. According to this analysis, being disliked by others isn't necessarily intrinsically painful, and being liked by others isn't an end in itself. Rather, we respond to the opinion of others because it may dictate our getting or not getting the things we need to survive, and only secondarily do we respond because of any value inherent in the verbal statements of approval and disapproval.

This issue, however, isn't crucial. Whether you believe that we want to be liked solely because we have a need, or solely because of the material consequences of the approval, or some combination of these two, it is patently obvious that all people do attempt to avoid disapproval. In the remainder of this book, when it is stated that people want or need social approval from others, it will be a phrase of convenience that doesn't necessarily have to rule out any of the interpretations just mentioned.

# *4*

# "You Bastard," and Other Terms of Endearment

## *Knowing When to Do It*

Imagine that you're having a conversation with someone at a cocktail party—not discussing anything particularly important, just small talk, but you're doing most of the talking and, consequently, enjoying yourself immensely. Suddenly the other person stops listening to your story about yesterday's incredible experience (". . .So I turned to the Meter Maid and said. . .") and calls out to someone walking nearby, immediately initiating a conversation with the newcomer and ignoring you. This party isn't fun any more.

You've been left with a dangling story and no "excuse me."

If the deserter was someone you just met, you've probably written her or him off, attributing to that person no class, no manners, an acute lack of perception, and no taste. Imagine, not even an "excuse me"!

Of course, it's not only strangers who suffer from lapses of class, manners, perception, and taste. If the offender was your spouse, lover, or close friend, chances are the incident will not pass without further remark, like immediately after the last farewell to your hostess ("Great party. Thank you." *The door closes.* "How dare you?!"). After the necessary recriminations, pouting, and just plain anger, the exchange will probably get down to your saying, "It wouldn't have been so bad if you had warned me, or if you'd apologized. But no, that's too much for you to do! You don't really care about me or how I feel. NO, DON'T TOUCH ME!"

The idea that the other person doesn't care is based on both the fact that you were abandoned and that you weren't given a social justification. You were treated as though you were unimportant—not worthy of an "excuse me." You're angry because you want it known that you will not tolerate being treated in such a disrespectful fashion.

If you can forget about your anger for a moment and instead analyze this situation, you will find an important element of the justification process. The logic which seems to be the basis of the anger is:

1. I am important.
2. Important people deserve justifications, but unimportant people don't.
3. I didn't receive a justification. Therefore, I'm being treated as unimportant and I won't stand for it.

That second assumption is the one that is of primary interest here: important people deserve social justifications and unimportant people don't. Therefore, we don't always justify; we take into account who it is that has decided that our behavior was inappropriate. If we consider the person to be a VIP, then we will definitely offer a social justification, and possibly two or three. But if we decide that the person is not important—not important to us at the moment, that is—then we probably won't justify.

For example, a woman, just out of law school, has been hired by a rather traditional (stuffy) law firm. On her third day on the job she works past normal quitting time. Eventually she begins to feel tired and drowsy and decides to slip off her shoes and rest her feet on the desk. It's late and there are not many people around and besides, it's her office. So, when a custodian comes in to empty the waste-paper basket, she doesn't move or even acknowledge his mumbled greeting. However, if it were one of the firm's senior partners who slipped in unannounced, it is entirely likely that she would quickly take her feet down and would just as hurriedly justify her overly relaxed manner ("I was just puzzling over the Jones case and my foot fell asleep . . .").

Similarly, if you answer the doorbell dressed in a dirty T-shirt and torn pants, you may or may not justify your appearance, depending on the caller's importance to you. If it is merely the newspaper boy, collecting his monthly bill, you probably won't justify ("Here's an extra quarter for you, kid"). But, if the person at the door is a new neighbor, one you have been trying to impress, then you'll probably fall all over yourself justifying (e.g., "I've just been trying to fix the plumbing," or "Oh, hi. I was just going to try out for 'Let's Make a Deal.' Do you think Monty will like it?").

So, it's how important we consider a person to be that

determines whether we justify. But what factors determine whom we consider to be important and therefore worthy of our explanations? At first glance it may seem that by definition it is the people we "like" who are important. But then the issue becomes *why* do we "like" them. For starters, the people we like are people who make us feel good; they have the ability to do things which give us pleasure. Because they have this capacity, we become attached to them and—in many ways—dependent upon them. Note that in this context the concept of dependency doesn't have any negative psychological connotations (i.e., he has a dependent personality, or she's a weak person, not independent enough). Rather, to say that we're dependent on someone simply describes the fact that we, like all other humans, get rewards and/or pleasure from another person. There is nothing inherently wrong with depending on others for some rewards, and indeed it is impossible in contemporary life to do otherwise.

"Liking," of course, is not a necessary component of dependency. We can talk about the people on whom we are dependent for rewards as "important" because they have the power to give us, or help us get, some of the things we need to survive. In the previous example, the young attorney perceived the senior partner as very important (i.e., controlling promotions, raises, and connections) and therefore someone deserving her justifications. The custodian was viewed as unimportant (he doesn't control valuable rewards), hardly deserving her recognition, much less a justification.

Whether or not we perceive ourselves as dependent on someone can vary from one situation to the next. For example, it is not necessarily the case that the custodian will always be seen as less "powerful" than the senior partner. What if the next day the young attorney realizes that she may have mistakenly thrown an important document into the wastebasket? Suddenly the custodian will become very important. The attorney will be very dependent on him because he has the power to decide whether or not to let her root through the giant trash bin in the basement of the building. Since it is now very important that the custodian "like" her so that he will help her, the attorney will now be exceptionally nice to him. As she rushes down the hall after him she shouts, "Excuse me, Sir!" No longer is he a nonentity, he is "Sir," the kind and helpful (and important) custodian. "I'm sorry to trouble you, Sir, but I think I mistakenly put an important document in the trash. I've been so nervous and exhausted as a result of starting this new job that I just can't keep things in order. Is there any way we can go through the trash to find that document? It's very important."

Chances are the custodian enjoys his suddenly elevated position, recognizes that it may be only temporary, and wants to make certain the attorney understands that in the future he should be treated with respect. So first he probably will talk about how difficult it will be to go searching around in the big trash container. He'll say that it's difficult, but he won't go so far as to say that it will be impossible. The young attorney understands that this response means that she must humble herself a little more. So she justifies her failure to speak to him earlier: "This new job has me so flustered that I don't even know what's going on around me. Why, you were in and out of my office yesterday before I even knew it. I hope I didn't seem rude—it's just this job. . . ."

So the attorney has apologized to the custodian, and the latter is assured of better treatment, for a few days at least. Chances are he won't find the document, his temporary power will be dissipated, but he probably will in the future get at least a cursory nod from the attorney.

The point of this example is that the amount of power a

particular person can have over us, and therefore our dependence on that person, may vary from time to time or from one situation to another. Typically, there are some people who seem to have power in almost all situations, and there are others who almost never find themselves in a situation in which they are "top dog." But, there is always a possibility that a power relationship may be completely reversed—temporarily, at least. Just as the attorney suddenly became very dependent on the custodian, it is conceivable that a situation might arise in which the senior partner could be very dependent on the young attorney (she might happen to overhear him making a shady "deal"). You just never know.

Of course, there are those "dog days" when it seems that everyone has power over you, that you are at least one step behind everyone else, being dragged along, totally dependent on the mercy of others. But then there are those days when you seem to have your act together—people are asking *your* opinion, seeking *your* favor and attention. Ah, it feels so good and it's fun while it lasts.

There are some social roles and situations in which being dependent on other people is an inherent and integral part of the scheme of things. With a nod toward overgeneralization, what follows is a partial list of those situations, the games we play in which social justification is inescapable, inevitable, and—in retrospect—part of the fun.

## NOVICES AND INITIATES

Almost by definition, newcomers to any situation (e.g., freshmen, new employees, Army recruits, new members of social groups or clubs, new residents of a community or apartment, visitors to a foreign country) are unaware of all the standards indigenous to the new situation. Additionally, they are surrounded by people who have experience and are therefore invested with power. Part of this power consists of the right to be offended at the novices' mistakes ("Oh, so you didn't know that the door is always to be locked behind you") and to make fun of them. Some particularly sadistic "oldsters" like to make a game of humiliating new "club" members by leading them into situations of inappropriate behavior and then watching them squirm as they socially justify.

## APPLICANTS

To apply for almost anything (e.g., a job, a loan, a scholar-ship, admission to a school or a social club) is to accept the burden of proving one's inherent value. We must frequently justify our past behavior that in the present context may be deemed socially inappropriate (e.g., "Why did you change residences so often last year?"). Most of us dislike these situations because we are at the mercy of another and must be prepared to justify everything we do or have done.

## FIRST-TIME SITUATIONS

Many situations—or their stereotyped versions—are virtually defined in terms of inappropriate behavior, or, at the very least, are characterized by great uncertainty about one's be-havior. The result is a kind of non-stop justification, an ex-planation of and apology for one's every move. Included in this category are such events as: the first date; the wedding night; the first time on the ski slopes; or the first time an individual appears publicly with a new hairstyle, a wig, a toupee, or a mustache. These situations have become such a cliché of our culture that simply because a justification is expected results in one being given, whether called for or not.

## SALESPEOPLE

Salespeople spend more time winning the approval of customers than they do actually selling. They are clearly dependent on being liked by their customers, and they are always meeting new people whose values and standards are not fully known. As a result, the good salespeople become particularly adept at searching for signals of disapproval from the potential customer and then quickly justifying their behavior or opinions. They must make the customer like them at all costs.

Salespeople are good examples of the earlier point that social justifications occur as a function of whether *another person* considers an action inappropriate, and not whether the individual himself considers his own action inappropriate. In one situation a salesman may justify an action because a customer defines it as inappropriately liberal or informal (to a conservative executive: "I apologize for being dressed so casually, but I had to call at the golf course this morning"); in another situation, he justifies the same action because it is judged inappropriately conservative (to a "hip" advertising executive: "Please excuse my button-downed appearance, but I had to do my bank president act earlier today"). Many of the people who fail as salespeople are those who are insensitive to their customers' standards for behavior or who are incapable of tactfully or convincingly justifying their social actions.

## STUDENTS

Students are surrounded by people with power (teachers, parents, more advanced students) who are constantly scrutinizing their behavior. Given the vast number of standards that can be applied, and the numerous authority figures to apply them, it is hardly surprising that students must become highly sophisticated at social justification. Poor grades, late assignments, tardiness, absenteeism, sloppy writing, cheating, and insufficient motivation are common inappropriate actions that must be justified in the academic sphere.

A student must also be concerned about how different groups of people will react to the same behavior. For example, getting high grades may please parents and teachers but be considered inappropriate by fellow students; hair and dress styles approved by other students are frequently deemed highly inappropriate by parents and principals; or pursuing an undergraduate major that does not lead to an immediate job upon graduation may be approved by professors but be considered a reflection of indirection and immaturity by parents.

## PATIENTS

Physicians frequently have an inordinate amount of discretionary social power and most patients approach them with some fear and trepidation. Patients guard against giving the impression that some action of their own may be the cause of their malady. Further, since many kinds of illnesses are lingering indicators of previous inappropriate behavior (e.g., venereal disease, liver ailments), and given the supposed importance of *not* engendering the doctor's disapproval, patients are usually on the defensive and have a repertoire of social justifications ready for any contingency.

The preceding list of situations, roles, and people characterized by extensive and laborious social justification is neither comprehensive nor universally inclusive. The primary focus of this list was on those times when we seem to be in situations of giving constant justifications. It should be remembered, however, that the people who are the recipients of these constant barrages of social justifications (e.g., police officers, bill collectors, judges, teachers, IRS employees, customs agents, and therapists) have their problems too. They are confronted by a world full of inappropriate behavior, all apparently caused by people who had nothing to do with it.

In addition to our degree of dependence on someone determining whether or not we'll offer a social justification, another important determinant is just how much the other person disapproves of our inappropriate behavior. If that person is really angry at us for our misdeeds, then it is much more likely that we'll justify than it would be if the person only shows mild annoyance. Because of this annoyance variable, it becomes crucial to understand exactly what determines how much people will disapprove of a particular inappropriate behavior.

One factor that obviously affects how someone will react to our ineptitude is the general relationship we have with that person. If the other person knows us pretty well, "understands" us, and likes us, then he probably won't get as angry with us as he would if he didn't know, "understand," or like us. Likewise, there are degrees of "liking" which affect the way one person may react to the same be-

havior from two individuals. In many cases this is reflected
as favoritism. An example is the Mom-always-liked-you-
better syndrome: Two children get mosquito bites which are
very itchy. The first child just puts a finger gently on one
bite to feel how much of a bump there is, and his mother
explodes into a high-volume lecture on "I told you not to
itch them." The other child has scratched the bites so much
that she has turned them into virtual open wounds. The parent doesn't condemn this child with ranting and raving, but
instead expresses sympathy and understanding about how
itchy and painful those nasty old mosquito bites must be.

Just as there are parents who play favorites, so too
there are bosses, teachers, co-workers, relatives, friends,
and even judges who consider an action to be extremely inappropriate if performed by someone—or a class of
someones—they don't like, while the identical behavior may
not even be considered in error when committed by one of
their favorite people. It is those people, the ones who are
already disliked, who get the greatest criticism for their actions and who, as a result, must be continually thinking up
appropriate justifications. If you are in someone's good
graces, then you can count on that positive bond to minimize the amount of disapproval generated in that other person by your inappropriate behavior. Using that affection as a
guide, you may be able to markedly decrease the frequency
and intensity of your justifications. In an optimal situation
you may be able to eliminate justifications altogether.

Another factor that affects the amount of disapproval
generated by our inappropriate behavior is the importance of
the violated standard to the other person. The more important a particular standard is to the observer of our behavior,
the more inappropriate our errant action will be deemed, and
the greater the resultant disapproval. If the other person
thinks the most important value in life involves a particular

standard of behavior, then even the most minor violation will result in an overkill of disapproval. For example, with Mr. Killawat, who believes that wasting electricity is second only to murder on the list of heinous crimes, the simple act of leaving a light on, even if you've only gone into another room for a few seconds and plan to return directly, will probably result in total condemnation. But then, we all have different ideas about what is important in life and in interpersonal behavior, and each of us therefore holds various expectations about what standards should never be violated.

Some of us worry about money, others worry about cleanliness and order, others about honesty and love, still others worry about sex. To the person who is consumed with "not wasting money," the simple act of buying some luxury item, like cologne or real cream, or adding an extra 1 or 2 percent to a tip may bring out a wrathful lecture about our frivolity and a recital of the reasons why we'll never be successful in life. To someone else, our minor indulgence might go unnoticed, or even result in praise. People who worry about honesty will criticize any statements or actions that hint of mendacity, while people who worry about cleanliness seem only too eager to express their opinions regarding the appearance or neatness of our house, office, car, or our own physical selves.

Because of this great diversity in how much different standards are valued by different people, one of the first orders of business when getting to know someone is to establish which standards are important to them and which are not. Once we ascertain this vital bit of information, we can exercise discretion and caution in those areas of behavior which are relevant to the other person's pet peeves, and we likewise can be more relaxed and casual in those behavioral domains that our acquaintance doesn't seem to care about.

Another factor affecting the response to an inappropriate behavior is the intent behind it. There is a general tendency to get much angrier about intended actions than about unintended actions, probably deriving from concern over whether or not the offending behavior will be repeated. If, as we sit there in our new double knit suit, we think that someone else's comment to the effect that anyone who wears polyester clothes has comparably synthetic tastes, was intentionally directed at us, we will disapprove a great deal. This disapproval is designed to get a prompt apology or justification, but more significantly to warn the caustic bastard that if he says that kind of thing again, there will be real trouble. Intended inappropriate behaviors, if unchecked by disapproval, could become commonplace. And so they must be nipped in the bud.

Doesn't it really irritate you when you've warned somebody that you don't like some particular thing (like gum chewing, cigarette smoking, knuckle cracking), and then within a matter of minutes or hours, they do it again? They either act as though they hadn't heard you, or if they had heard, then they don't seem to care. And when someone who is supposed to care doesn't, then we are usually very quick to find it out. To do this we may set up a little test in which we get really angry, and then watch the response. For example, we may say something like, "I can't believe you did that! Don't you know that it upsets me very much? It's clear you don't really care about me. I can't maintain a relationship with someone who doesn't respect my feelings." That final threat to sever relations represents an exceptionally high level of disapproval of the other person's inappropriate behavior. It also represents the crucial element in our test of whether the truth resides in the other person's words that he cares, or in his actions which seem to be saying that he doesn't. If he responds by offering a good justification, we give him a reprieve, more secure now in our belief that he does care. On the other hand, he may say, "Well, if that's the way you feel about it, I guess there's no use talking about it. You obviously don't think much of our relationship. I mean, if you want to end our whole relationship over one little thing, what can I say?" This response obviously is not what we had hoped for, because it indicates that we were correct in our suspicion. Now the ball is back in our court and we must decide whether or not to live up to our threat.

We'll have to leave that decision in abeyance, because the purpose of this example is simply to illustrate another factor that determines the degree or intensity of disapproval generated by what we consider to be an inappropriate behavior. That factor is the number of times the person has done it and whether or not we have warned him that we think the behavior is inappropriate. We might not get very upset the first time someone does something we dislike, and we may even let it pass the second time. But if he has done it several times and we have warned him that we don't like it, then we may be very strong in our disapproval. And, in general, the greater our disapproval, the more likely it is that the other person will offer a justification in an effort to make amends.

Another consideration is the degree of inappropriateness of the action, at least from our subjective point of view. Given the fact that a behavior can fail to fit or match a standard either by a little or a lot, then we can reasonably assume that the more a behavior fails to match a standard, the greater will be the disapproval. For example, the standard that dictates promptness can be violated by a small deviation (being 6 minutes late) or by a large deviation (not showing up at all). Similarly, you can put your whole foot in your mouth or only your little toe.

Closely related to the degree of discrepancy is the

amount of pain or damage that results from the behavior. Our forgetfulness can result in the loss of a big sales contract, or in the ruination of twenty dollars' worth of steaks, or in the destruction of somebody's feelings of self-worth. Of course, we could get lucky and somebody else could catch our error, remind us that the steaks are on the grill, or soften the effect of our inconsiderate comments. Thus, exactly the same behavior might have dire consequences in one situation, but do little or no damage in another situation. In general, the greater the amount of damage that is caused by the inappropriate behavior, the greater the resultant disapproval. Or, as basketball announcers sometimes say, "No harm, no foul." If the contract isn't lost, the steaks aren't cremated on the grill, or the other person isn't offended, humiliated, or otherwise in need of a medic, then the inappropriate behavior won't result in a significant amount of disapproval. The behavior will probably still be judged as inappropriate, but it just won't be disapproved of as much.

Another way to state this is to say that the "wrongness" of a behavior depends as much on the consequences or outcome of that behavior as it does on the behavior in and of itself. This is often confusing to children. For example, they are told that it is wrong to tell lies, but then they see that adults act as though it is all right to lie to one another, just as long as no one is "hurt." While we often say we have strict principles and values, we have so many values that they are often in conflict and therefore making judgments is sometimes difficult and confusing. Although we value honesty, we also value not hurting someone's feelings or not wasting money. Thus, we might not tell the whole truth to the IRS (if the whole truth would result in added taxes for us), or we might not admit that we like someone if our conversation partner dislikes that someone.

In each of these instances we might argue that our lack of truthfulness wasn't so bad because "no one was hurt by it," or "no harm was done."

In sum, these six factors (i.e., relation to the person, importance of the standard, intent, frequency, degree of inappropriateness, and amount of damage) can all contribute to the total amount of disapproval which results from an inappropriate behavior. Further, the two primary determinants of whether or not someone will offer a social justification for an inappropriate behavior are (1) the amount of disapproval from the other person, and (2) the degree of dependency on the other person (i.e., the person's importance). In general, as the amount of disapproval and degree of dependency increase, so will the likelihood of a social justification.

There is one important exception to the idea that a person's tendency to justify increases directly with the amount of the other's disapproval. When the level of disapproval reaches extremely high levels, the likelihood of justifying may drop rather dramatically. At first, it may seem as though the most obvious time to expect justifications would be if someone was being strongly criticized. But, upon closer analysis, it is evident that there are several other factors that need to be considered.

Most of us won't undertake something that we think will ultimately be futile. If you have just blundered and made someone really dislike you, your chances aren't very promising for coming up with a justification that will quell all that anger. And, since it's unlikely that your justification will succeed, there's very little point in even offering one. You may as well save your breath, bear the disapproval, and figure out some way to salvage the relationship.

If you are just getting to know someone, you may be reluctant to justify if she criticizes you too strongly, because you consider her extreme reaction to be inappropriate. That is, you decide that she has behaved inappropriately by making such an excessively critical evaluation of your previous action. As a result of judging her act of disapproval to be inappropriate, you attribute some undesirable traits to her (e.g., hot-headed, super-sensitive, thinks she's God) and conclude that you don't want her as a friend. You may end up disapproving of her action so much that you decide that if that is the kind of person she is, then she isn't worth your time and energy. Thus, based on her excessive disapproval, you reach the verdict that she isn't really important to you, that you won't be dependent on her, and that you don't care whether she likes you—so you don't justify at all.

If you're not willing to end a new-found relationship simply because the other person was very harsh on you, there is still another reason not to justify. By justifying after someone has just dumped on you, you are implicitly acknowledging his right to make and verbalize such extreme judgments again in the future. Your justification legitimizes his behavior regardless of whether or not it successfully reduces his feelings of disapproval. In terms of power in the relationship, you will have lost out even if you win back his approval. You have lost power because the other person now has the right to be a harsh judge, capable of making scathing indictments of your character. Rather than give this kind of privilege to the other person, especially in the initial stages of a relationship, it is better not to justify. In fact, we might even call the other person's behavior into question: "Look, it's okay for me to say that kind of thing about myself, but I haven't given you permission to do it." Thus, rather than justify after extreme disapproval, we protect our future power in the relationship by not justifying and thereby possibly even challenging the other person.

# II

# HOW WE DO IT

# 5

# No, What I Meant Was. . .

## *Working with the Behavior, and Trying to Make It Go Away*

What do you do if you have just been caught with your foot in your mouth or your eyes on someone else's spouse? There you were, behaving in a socially inappropriate fashion, and you got nailed in the act. Without any words being said, you just know that the observer's standard for proper conduct has been applied, and you have been found wanting. You sway from a sense of lightheadedness; there is a vague feeling of nausea stirring in your lower abdomen. Is there no graceful way out of this situation? Of course there is: you justify!

This is a tricky situation, however. Just any old justification won't do. Since you did it, and you were seen doing it, and you definitely don't want to own up to it, you have to somehow convince the other person that he misperceived the whole thing, that his conception of what happened isn't what happened at all. You have to convince him that your behavior was in no way inconsistent with his standard. Sound difficult? It really isn't—we do it all the time.

The approach called for here involves working with the other person's definition of what behavior actually took place. In essence, this strategy attempts to alter the other person's very definition of reality. The other person may think that one thing really happened, but your social justification will introduce information which challenges that conception of reality by substituting a different and vastly more favorable definition of "what really happened." Remember, though, that in employing this technique there is no attempt to question the validity of the standard which is being applied to the behavior in question. For example, "Now look. If I had lied to you, then you would have every reason to be angry with me. But I didn't really lie. What I said was. . ."

These types of justifications typically require a fair amount of ingenuity, poise, and dexterity. You must quickly find just the right thing to do or say so that you can immediately convince the other person that he or she was in error in thinking you had done something inappropriate when in "fact" what you just did was entirely normal. In its most extreme form, this technique includes complete denial that the behavior ever occurred. To do this effectively, it is necessary to convince the observer that even though he thinks he noted some untoward behavior, the truth is that his senses are deceiving him because NOTHING HAPPENED.

This magic act of "first you see it, now you don't"

relies heavily on the speed with which certain things occur. Some behaviors (such as small burps, yawns, flatulence, and brief moments of extreme awkwardness) pass very quickly. And because they do happen so quickly, the person skilled in this form of justification can, by his demeanor, act as though *nothing ever happened*.

For example, imagine a diplomat who drinks a Dr. Pepper just prior to a formal dinner. At the table he is seated next to a head of state and an ambassador; the three of them are talking genially and politely, enjoying the first course of dinner. And then it happens: the Dr. Pepper runs its course and the unfortunate diplomat burps—a small and discreet burp, to be sure, but undeniably a burp. So what does the diplomat do?

1. Become embarrassed?
2. Murmur apologies?
3. Mumble, "It must have been that Dr. Pepper"?
4. Frown and gently punch his stomach?
5. Run screaming from the room?
6. Resign his post?

No. He takes none of these options. Instead he continues talking and eating his soup, just as though nothing had happened. His manner suggests that everything is normal and leaves his companions mentally questioning whether or not what they heard was, in fact, a burp.

In less formal circumstances this technique can be embellished somewhat with usually satisfactory results. Instead of ignoring this social faux pas, the perpetrator will cast a quick glance of mild surprise and/or disapproval at an unsuspecting bystander (perhaps even Fido) as if to say to any onlookers, "Well, really! . .Did you hear what I heard? I would never do that."

The technique of total denial is usually the most satis-factory option, however, since it doesn't even leave room for guilt-by-association. And it does have everyday, practi-cal applications. It has even been observed at the local ham-burger stand. A harried father tries to carry ten dollars' worth of Big Macs, Small Fries, Cokes, and Ronald Mac-Donald paste-ups to his family waiting in the car. One of the soft drinks falls to the pavement with a magnificent splash, but the man just keeps on walking. Only those closely scrutinizing this clumsy performance could tell from his unchanged demeanor that anything had happened, and even they might be unable to determine if *he* was aware of it.

This ability to ignore the minor calamities of life is a necessary part of training for the professional performer. Ac-tors who forget their lines just keep going until they get back on the right track. A pianist may skip a full sixteen bars, but her face will never show it. This technique can also be observed in active conversations. A man may begin to interject a statement by saying "Ahh. . .," but suddenly realize that what he was about to say would be stupid or irrelevant. So when his partner in conversation finishes her sentence, she may defer to him and say, "You were about to say. . .?" The man's response is a surprised, "Oh! No, I didn't say anything."

This "nothing happened" technique works best either when the behavior is very brief or when the observer didn't get a good chance to fully see or hear the action. As a de-vice for social justification, it is very effective, since if there was no behavior to begin with, then obviously there is no-thing to be compared to a standard and judged inappro-priate. Typically, of course, the observer did see the inci-dent, but decides not to make an issue of it.

Occasionally people will try to adapt the "nothing happened" technique to a fairly extended behavior sequence. A coed, for example, may spend a night at her boyfriend's apartment, but when questioned by her mother—who had, of course, tried to call her—she will maintain that she was in the dormitory, but was on another floor, helping a girlfriend study for an exam. Or a boss may not be able to find one of his employees, and suspects that he has taken an unscheduled break. When confronted, however, the employee says, "I don't know *why* you couldn't find me. I was there all the time. Did you check the supply room?"

## I WAS ONLY FIXING MY HAIR

Another clever strategy for subtly justifying a behavior involves *embedding* that behavior in a larger, more extended sequence of actions. Imagine an action is committed which, if taken by itself, is clearly inappropriate. In an attempt to avoid its detection, several more actions are added so that the behavioral unit is then defined in terms of a longer sequence.

Let's look again at an example touched on earlier. A woman is late getting to the airport to meet an old friend. She knows the plane has already landed, so she walks quickly down the corridor toward the arrival gate. Thinking she sees her friend walking toward her in the mass of deplaned passengers, she raises her hand to wave a greeting. Just as her hand reaches its apogee, the other person looks straight at her and it isn't her friend at all. After only the slightest hesitation, the eye contact is broken and the hand, which was all primed to wave, is slowly lowered to adjust an imaginary stray hair.

By including this additional action—smoothing her hair—the woman attempts to transform the observer's conception of what actually happened. This is not an act of someone presumptuously waving at a stranger. Rather it is an innocuous act of grooming. In fact, many unsuccessful attempts to flag cabs or to attract inattentive waiters are eventually transformed into acts of personal hygiene. Of course, one act of personal hygiene may be embedded in another. A man raises his arm, turns his head slightly, and adjusts his hair. During that brief head turn, he takes a deep breath to check if his Ban Roll-on is still doing its job.

In the same airport terminal, a fairly distinguished look-ing middle-aged man pauses for a few seconds to stare at the shapely posterior of a young woman who is standing at the paperback bookrack. When the woman moves on, the man blinks and realizes that a salesperson has been watching him all the time. His response—a sheepish grin? No, never! He refocuses his eyes and with a look of intense concentra-tion, walks over to the bookrack, picks up a book, and examines its cover and contents. The additional action of going to pick up the book is intended to communicate to the salesclerk that he is not a dirty old man staring. To the con-trary, that whole time his mind was focused on higher, more intellectual matters. In this non-verbal interchange with the clerk, the man embeds his inappropriate behavior in a longer behavioral unit which is not inconsistent with any standard.

In the classroom, many students become expert social justifiers through the use of this embedding technique. Dur-ing examinations, students occasionally glance at the papers of adjacent test-takers. As soon as the student becomes aware that the teacher is observing him, he will rotate his head backward and begin rubbing his neck. By adding these actions, the student attempts to define his wayward glance as merely the first part of the more extended behavioral unit of relaxing a sore neck. The sore neck routine does have the virtue of additional veracity, since hunching over writing on a desk for an extended period can produce some muscle strain. In a somewhat similar way, a student who raises her hand to answer a question, and then realizes her answer is incorrect, may raise the other arm and act as though she is actually stretching.

Teachers also have developed an embedding technique for justifying incorrect lecture statements. If a perceptive student points out that a statement by the teacher contradicts the textbook or a previous lecture, the teacher is likely to say, "I just said that to make sure you were paying attention." By adding this statement, the teacher attempts to transform the error into a part of a more extended behavioral sequence, which will not only justify the mistake but which may also enhance her reputation as a clever classroom lecture strategist.

Likewise, an individual who trips while walking may feign several more trips and explain that he is only practicing his trip. Remarkable! What looked like clumsiness is actually an example of a potential actor practicing his art! Freeway drivers who discover they have left their turn signal blinking for the past half mile after a change of lanes, sometimes change lanes one more time and then turn off the blinker. Through this prolonged sequence, their action indicates prudence and caution rather than laxity and poor driving habits. While driving along a city street, a long-haired young man passes a couple of hitchhikers, equally long tressed. He quickly puts on his turn signal. By adding the turn signal routine he embeds his inconsiderateness toward fellow travelers in a longer sequence, thereby explaining it away.

This embedding technique can also be observed in conversations. Imagine an important business conference in which all of the participants are actively discussing which approach to adopt toward some thorny problem. After twenty minutes of heated conversation, one of the participants offers what is clearly the best solution and one which is also clearly in direct conflict with an earlier proposal. In order to save face, the person who made that earlier proposal will probably say something like, "Yeah, that's exactly what I was trying to get at earlier, but I never got a chance to finish explaining." He will then proceed to repeat his earlier comment and go on to show how his idea "logically" leads to the same solution. This is actually more a case of "embellishing" than it is of "embedding." Viewed in retrospect, however, the initial inept comment is supposed to be seen as part of a more extended sequence, and as such is neither inappropriate nor in any way indicative of his lack of creative insight.

## WELL, IT COULD HAVE BEEN WORSE!

Another common technique of social justification involves setting up a contrast between the behavior that occurred and the behavior that *could have* occurred. When we do something inappropriate, and sense the disapproval of others present, we may then describe a *really* inappropriate action which we didn't do. By comparison to this potential catastrophe, our inappropriate action is supposed to pale to insignificance.

Dieters often employ this contrast technique. A woman on a strict diet just can't resist ordering a piece of apple pie for dessert. As she finishes giving her order to the waiter, she looks at her luncheon companion and sees a shocked and puzzled expression. The dieter's response? "Well, it could have been worse! At least I didn't order Strawberry Shortcake, 'smothered in rich and sensuous mounds of fresh whipped cream,' and I didn't order Fannie's Famous Fudge Cake, 'a rich and tempting blend of French and Swiss chocolates, saturated with rum and topped off with minced sugared walnuts.' It could have been worse—*a lot* worse! I could have ordered one of those!''

Likewise, an older child, when being scolded by a parent, justifies hitting her younger brother by asserting, ''But I didn't hit him hard.'' Smokers sometimes justify their habit by pointing out that if they didn't smoke they would put on weight and that would be a worse evil. In a reverse tactic, a heavy eater will occasionally argue that the only way he can stop eating so much would be to start smoking, and we all know that would be even worse.

The phrase ''better late than never'' captures the essence of another application of the contrast technique—the justification of tardiness. As a social justification the implication is, ''Well, it could have been worse. What if I hadn't shown up at all?'' Once again we are trying to alter the observer's point of view, thereby reducing or eliminating the disapproval.

And one more: Encountering a fellow conventioneer whom she just met the previous day, a woman points her finger, and with a quizzical tone says, ''Martin?'' The annoyed reply, ''No, it's Marion.'' In a move that is somewhat akin to grasping at straws, the woman says, ''Well, at least I got the first letter right.'' And this remark is designed, of course, to point out just how bad her memory could have been, and thereby minimize the error.

Another variation of this technique is to contrast our present inappropriate behavior with the ''unspeakable'' way we used to act. (''You think I'm shy *now;* you should have seen me before I took the Dale Carnegie course!'') The contrast technique is also evident when we attempt to socially justify our actions by pointing out that someone else has done something that is much more inappropriate. Children are experts at this. (''But Johnny hit him *three* times!'')

This tactic of pointing a finger at somebody else is not confined exclusively to children. For example, a woman at a cocktail party is introduced to someone, and in the course of their somewhat formal exchange she happens to reveal that she is the mother of six children. Noting a surprised expression on the other person's face, she snaps back, "I don't think that's so many. A neighbor of mine has ten." In this example the other person's expression of surprise actually resulted from amazement that the woman still had such a good figure. The woman, however, was operating on the assumption that her behavior was being implicitly questioned and unfavorably evaluated. She responded as though she were being criticized for adding to the population problem. Her own paranoia turned a compliment into an attack.

A more devious and less productive version of the contrast technique is to point out that your behavior isn't as bad as, or at least no worse than the behavior of the person who is criticizing you. For example, upon being criticized for being impatient and intolerant of others, you might say, "And look who's talking about tolerance, and with her every breath is criticizing me! You're worse than I am! Practice what you preach, Dearie." Please note that although this variation will seldom reduce the other person's disapproval, it will serve as a diversionary tactic to at least get attention shifted away from our faults and/or errors.

Normally our use of the contrast technique requires a verbal description of the more extreme inappropriate behavior which could have occurred. This is not always necessary, however—the contrast technique can also be executed nonverbally. In this instance, the person who has committed the inappropriate act doesn't make any overt response, but instead acts as though *nothing really significant* has happened. This non-response is designed to imply that while the inappropriate behavior did occur, it wasn't of sufficient significance to warrant concern. The implicit message to the observer is, "Sure, I did it, but it wasn't any big deal, so don't disapprove of me."

For example, Norm is driving Fred to the football game. Now Norm is the kind of guy who likes to look you in the eye when he's talking to you—even when he's driving. Fred, however, prefers to keep his eyes on the road, even if he is not the driver. And so Norm, who is busily describing his favorite football player, goes right through an intersection without seeing or slowing down for the stop sign, and has to swerve wildly to miss a car coming out of the side street—none of which interferes with his story of football heroics. He ignores Fred's terrified reaction (he has jammed his foot onto an imaginary brake, put his hands over his face, and is on his twelfth "Hail Mary") and continues talking and driving as though the incident were nothing at all. The implication of Norm's casual approach is that there was no danger, that this sort of thing happens all the time, and therefore there was no cause for alarm.

The contrast technique Norm employed didn't involve any verbal comment about how bad the behavior could have been. Instead, Norm's contained demeanor implied that the whole thing was "no big deal." In fact, if Norm had made a comment, the justification technique might not have worked. If, for example, he had waited until he had driven another block and then said something like, "Kind'a close, huh?" or "Had you a little worried on that one, didn't I?" instead of further minimizing the inappropriateness of his behavior, it would have allowed Fred a perfect opportunity to rejoin with something like, "Close, my eye! You almost got us killed back there!"

## I KNOW IT MAY SEEM THAT WAY, BUT. . .

Does the Wednesday night bingo session at the local church represent a devious way of gambling, or does it simply provide an amusing and relaxing (and painless) way to donate money to a worthy cause?

There are many behaviors—gambling with bingo is only one—which might be defined as illegal, immoral, or inappropriate from one point of view, but which might be seen as entirely proper and acceptable from another. And herein lies another form of social justification: the "I know it may seem that way, but what I really was doing was this. . ." explanation. ("Don't you see, playing bingo is nothing more than my way of tithing. After all, there's no rule that says being charitable can't be fun.") The attempt here is to introduce a new definition, to redefine the behavior for the observer.

For example, a young woman is standing in the entranceway of a restaurant. As each new group of customers comes in, she conspicuously looks at her watch, sighs, and shifts her weight from one foot to another. Rather than have her act of waiting interpreted as in any way inappropriate, she communicates—nonverbally—to all who pass by that she is not at fault here, that she is standing there for perfectly legitimate reasons, and that somebody else is being really inappropriate by not being there on time ("I'm not loitering, I'm waiting; I'm not early, he's late").

Or, imagine that after a long day at the office the boss invites Paul to his house for a drink, a really special concoction, based on his own secret recipe. Paul takes his first swallow, gasps, gulps, and grabs his neck. The boss says, "What's the matter? Don't you like it?" Realizing that it would be unwise to proclaim his true feelings on the subject, Paul replies, "Oh, no, great drink, great drink... I just have a tickle in my throat. It's probably from that smoky conference room and having to talk all day. No, no, the drink is good. Really good. I've never tasted anything quite like it." And so saying, he takes another sip from his rum martini gimlet. If he is lucky, Paul will have changed his boss's perception of what happened, so that what seemed like an inappropriate reaction to an inappropriate drink is redefined as a behavior common to one who has worked so diligently under somewhat trying circumstances.

By using the *redefinition* technique, we try to change the observer's conception of the nature of the behavior that occurred. The goal is to redefine the behavior so that it is not inappropriate or inconsistent with any standards for behavior that may be held by the observer. Through this technique a blunt and gauche remark is turned into one that is ironic, satirical, or metaphoric, but certainly nothing that would offend. Likewise *Playboy* is described as a serious literary journal and *Screw* as an attempt to understand the current counterculture.

The redefinition technique of justification is widely used in diplomatic circles. Statements to the press are routinely worded in a very ambiguous manner so that they can be reinterpreted should something new develop. The diplomat can always redefine his statement so that he does not appear to be guilty of inconsistency or deception. After all, that's what diplomacy is all about.

Politicians also find this device useful when they endorse a bill that seems inconsistent with their stated values or past behavior. One senator recently commented that "*in essence* this measure is no different from several earlier bills that have been passed in the Congress." His constituents are supposed to look at the *essence* of the bill, rather than at its overt language. In reality, he has probably compromised his values and is trying to socially justify his behavior through the process of redefinition.

Many of our behaviors consist of both external bodily movement and internal mental activity. Since the exact nature of our internal activity cannot be directly observed, it is sometimes very difficult to specify exactly what we have been doing. The redefinition technique often relies on this ambiguity. A man goes to a concert and during the first movement of the first piece, he closes his eyes for a few minutes. Receiving a nudge from his wife, he snorts, frowns, and says, "I was listening. I just closed my eyes so that I could concentrate better on the music."

Whether the technique is the *denial* that the behavior actually occurred, *embedding* the action in a longer behavioral sequence and thereby rendering it okay, *contrasting* our behavior to what could have been much worse, or *defining* our behavior so that it does not seem inappropriate, we all rely on it at some time or another. We accept the standard the observer is applying ("You're right, gambling is a bad thing"), but we try to alter the perception of exactly what we have done. The execution is sometimes tricky, but when properly done the result can be effective.

# 6

# Don't Look at Me, I Didn't Do It

*Working with the Standard, and Trying to Change It*

But what if we can't change other people's perception of what happened? They saw, their standard was applied, and our behavior was found to be inappropriate. So what can we do? Let's see now—if we are being disapproved of because one of our behaviors isn't consistent with another person's standard for that behavior, then what if we try to get that person to use a different standard? If we can get the observer to do this, to use a standard with which the behavior is congruent, then that person won't be able to judge our behavior as inappropriate, and therefore can't legitimately disapprove of us! That's it! All we have to do is convince the other person that he is using the wrong standard!

In using this general approach to social justification, we accept the fact that the behavior occurred in the way the observer thinks. However, we introduce evidence to persuade our judge that although his perception of the behavior is correct, the standard he is using to judge us is incorrect. By presenting evidence about some of the "extenuating circumstances" in the situation, we try to get him to evaluate our behavior by comparison with a standard that is slightly different, slightly more lenient than the one he was using.

This approach is founded on the fact that people's initial judgments of behavior are typically based on broad and all-inclusive standards. This is the case since most standards are formulated in a very general way, and *supposedly* apply to all people, at all times, in all places, under all varieties of conditions. For example, the standard concerning honesty specifies that an individual should *always* be honest, and the standard concerning promptness requires that one should *always* be right on time.

How do we change these standards so that what we did will be all right? Take the "cleanliness" standard as an example. This standard in its broadest application says that we should be neat and clean and smell sweet like soap at all times. This general standard can, however, be temporarily replaced with a sub-standard which is a little more lenient, one that allows some slight deviation. For example, while doing some job around the house—like gardening, scrubbing the floor, painting, tye-dying your sneakers—it is entirely likely (and logical) that you might get soiled. What we have to do in this case, in terms of justifying our appearance, is to point out the extenuating circumstances which dictate that some sub-variety of the basic standard be used in making any judgment of our behavior. In other words, we have to show the observer why it is necessary to forgo the general standard which requires us to be immaculate at all times, and instead to apply a sub-standard which allows us to be at least a little bit messy.

For example, under normal conditions no self-respecting man or woman would allow themselves to be seen walking around in dirty, smelly clothes. But what if they had just finished playing tennis, or jogging, or exercising at Jack LaLanne's? Under those circumstances, such a physical state would be not only conceivable, but excusable, and a corresponding substandard would be applied, one which allowed the person to be grubby—at least for a while. Typically, you can get away with wearing your exercise outfit for half-an-hour or so, but then you will have to get out of it. However, while passing through the house, on the way to the shower, the athlete may be permitted briefly to stand or even to sit—but only on the edge of the chair—to watch some major TV event. The additional sub-standard applied here ("Well, pro-bowling *is* his favorite program") allows that the suspension of the cleanliness standard be extended for a few minutes. It must be noted, however, that this extension is only temporary, and the person who invokes it would do well not to push his luck. The showers are inevitable, pro-bowling or no.

Basically, then, the sub-standard, while effective, is only a temporary measure giving the offender an opportunity to mend his ways and correct his behavior. If this is not done within a reasonable period of time, the sub-standard will expire and the original standard will be reinstated. For example, we might excuse the poor work of an employee because of some personal problem she is experiencing, but there are limits to this tolerance. If her performance becomes too sloppy, or if it goes on for too long a time, we will soon be reapplying the general standard which demands a high level of performance.

The heart of the process invoking the sub-standard is the "extenuating circumstance." One can only marvel at the capacity of human beings for coming up with these extenuating circumstances that must be considered before any final judgments are made or verdicts are handed down. Most of us are absolutely ingenious at pointing out factors that make this particular situation different from others. And since it is different, then obviously the strict, general standard shouldn't be applied to our actions, at least not until we have had enough time to alter our behavior so that it is no longer inappropriate. Let's examine some of the more common examples of this approach.

## THAT WASN'T ME

One of the most frequently used justifications involves blaming someone else for our offending behavior. We are "only doing what they told us to do," and, in fact, it may as well be them carrying out these inappropriate behaviors. Children learn this technique very early (it's amazing what they pick up from watching television and parents)—"Nancy said she would beat me up if I didn't do it," or "I was only doing what Mommy told me. . . ." On the other end of the age spectrum, a seventy-year-old man at a supermarket checkout gives the cashier a handful of discount coupons. The cashier's face expresses distinct displeasure, and the other customers sigh as one and make vague menacing gestures. In an effort to stave off attack, the man says, "I don't know why my wife insists on saving these damn things. She always sticks me with cashing them in."

The function of this type of social justification is to

point out the extenuating circumstance that we are *only* doing what someone told us to do. By implicating another person, we suggest that our behavior is to be judged by a standard which takes into account the fact that our actions are to a great extent determined by another person. For example, look at the case of Fran. Her husband Henry asks her to take the car to the garage to get the fan belt fixed. At the garage the mechanic says, "Fan belt? You must be nuts, lady. It's not the fan belt. Your problem is the radiator." Sufficiently intimidated, Fran replies, "Well, I don't know anything about it. My husband said it was the fan belt, but I guess you'd better fix the radiator too." Later, when she recounts the episode to her husband, he explodes, "How can you be so guillible, so stupid! There was nothing wrong with the radiator." Her reply, "But, Henry, the man at the garage told me. . . ."

Not meaning to be too rough on Fran, it should be noted that one can easily be intimidated by people who are supposedly authorities in areas about which we know nothing. At the same time, however, we do too often abdicate responsibility in such circumstances by declaring, "I was only doing what I was told." This excuse of "simply following instructions" can be used to justify a lot of fumbled and inappropriate behaviors. Children of all ages justify inappropriate behavior by saying that their parents or older children made them do it ("But Mommy, you told me to always tell the whole truth. . ."). Husbands do what their wives tell them and wives do what their husbands tell them. Students only follow instructions. Employees put the responsibility on the boss ("He told me to clean out the files"). Patients justify their actions on the grounds that they are only following their doctor's advice ("I wish I could help with the chores, dear, but the doc did tell me to get a lot of rest"). Experts in all areas (e.g., mechanics, repair-

ers, salespeople, ministers, therapists—especially therapists)
are used by helpless non-experts as bases for socially justifying their own poor decisions and inappropriate behaviors.
The low level bureaucrat is only following the rules laid
down by the supervisor, who in turn is only carrying out the
orders of his supervisor, who, in turn, etc. This technique is
particularly popular in political circles and is known un-
officially as the "Watergate Syndrome."

Of course, this same "syndrome" works in reverse just
as easily and effectively. People with power are able to
exploit their position for purposes of justification: they rely
on the supposed incompetence of the people working under
them to excuse away their own inappropriate behavior. For
example, a boss will frequently justify his own stupidity,
negligence, or just plain irresponsibility on the grounds that
his secretary misplaced some papers, or didn't get a letter
out, or forgot to tell him about a phone call or an appointment. This tactic, however, demands care in the execution,
because a secretary scorned can get a boss in a lot of trouble. Likewise, a spouse, friend, or general peer may resent
being made the scapegoat for our own inappropriate behaviors, and may scream bloody murder, which only serves
to compound the inappropriateness of the whole affair. In
such cases it is best to fall back on the unsuspecting patsy.
For example, imagine a man standing in a somewhat disorganized waiting line. Through his impatience to get the
whole thing over with, he shoves the woman in front of
him. She turns, giving him a look of marked displeasure, so
he in turn casts a scornful glance at the person behind him,
who just stares blankly back. The shover then leans toward
the woman in front of him and confides: "I just can't understand some people. They have no patience at all; just
push and shove."

By far the most effective justification in the "It Wasn't

Me'' genre is the one by which we succeed in actually implicating the person who is disapproving of the behavior. Kids are pros at this, as noted earlier. Likewise adept are husbands and wives. Jim wants to watch the roller deby on TV, and so with only great reluctance does he agree to do the laundry. When June later starts sorting out the clean wash for ironing, she goes into an rage, screaming, "You washed little Johnny's red sweatshirt with my fine hand washables! Everything is pink!" To which Jim replies, "But Hon, you told me, 'Do the wash.' So I did the wash.''

## It's Not Me, It's Only My Body

We all seem to be experts at separating ourselves from our bodies. This puzzling distinction between self and body makes it possible for people to justify themselves by attributing an inappropriate behavior to some deficiency of their bodies. For example, a checkout clerk operating a cash register overcharges a customer for an item. The customer complains and points to the price sticker which clearly indicates the exact cost. The cashier replies, "Oops, you're right. I'm going to have to get glasses. I just can't see as well as I used to." The clerk has thereby implicated his body, dismissing any hint of carelessness or stupidity. This kind of justification implicitly says, "Don't judge me in terms of a standard applicable to a normally healthy person; instead use a standard that is appropriate for people who have deficient vision."

This same social justification can be communicated non-verbally. A pianist (using sheet music) is performing for a few friends. When she makes a mistake, she darts her head forward and squints her eyes. The implication is, "I made a mistake because *my eyes* aren't good enough to see the notes. They made the mistake; I didn't." In a similar manner, people reading to a group will sometimes quickly jerk the paper closer to their face after mispronouncing a word.

Of course, not everybody has bad eyes. Some people have bad ears: "Oh, I didn't hear you right, I thought you said. . . ." And some people have faulty hair: "I just can't do anything with this straight/curly, oily/dry hair of mine." Or it could be their hands: "With these stubby fingers of mine I just can't do that kind of intricate work." Or their feet: "My feet are so big, I'm always bumping into things." And sometimes it's the whole body: "If I weren't so tall/short, heavy/thin, I could do it."

Adolescent diseases and injuries which can and often do have permanent effects are frequently used to justify myriad unconnected acts of incompetence. After a golfer slices a drive into an adjacent fairway, he may comment, "I wish I'd never played football in high school. This shoulder of mine just hasn't been right ever since."

Permanent internal defects of the body are also useful for purposes of social justification. Few people say that they are overweight because *they* can't control how much they eat. They overeat because they have this "glandular problem." People say they have poor complexions because of an endocrine imbalance. People justify smoking and not stopping by complaining about a bodily craving, or about their "bad nerves" due to "pressures." "Internal physiological cravings" make some people horny and in constant need of sexual activity, while these same psychological factors make others completely uninterested and—sometimes—incapable.

Another frequent type of social justification involves a *temporary* illness, injury, or bodily disturbance. Everybody knows and uses these. The worker isn't performing up to par because of a cold, a headache, "personal problems," or a hangover. A common way to justify breaking an appointment, a date, or a party engagement is to cite illness. These illnesses frequently strike with lightning speed: "I'm sorry, but I won't be able to make it tonight. I was really planning to come. I was feeling fine when I left work, but all of a sudden I started feeling queasy in the stomach, got hot flashes, and my joints ache. So I guess we had better try for some other time." Of course, when asked a couple of days later how they feel, these social justifiers sometimes slip by saying, "Hunh? What do you mean? I've been fi. . . Oh! You mean the *other* night. . . ."

Some women occasionally justify being nervous, inconsiderate, or inconsistent by attributing their behavior to menstruation. (It should be noted that while this may indeed be a difficult time, some women admit to using the excuse perhaps a little more than is necessary.) And some periods seem to go on all month. And then there's "change-of-life"—both women and men use this one, although men are only recently realizing its full potential as a source of justifications.

Then there's the medicine that people take to get rid of the initial problem—sometimes the cure is worse than the disease: "These pills just knock me out." "I feel so groggy after taking that cough medicine." "When my doctor puts me on this stuff, it makes me so hyper I can't concentrate."

Many of us have encountered the reluctant pianist or singer who will agree to perform for us only after an opening exchange of two or three "Oh-I-couldn'ts." When the performer does finally agree to perform, she justifies all anticipated errors by disclaiming, "But I'm so out of practice. I just know I'll make a mess of it."

This example represents still another variation of the self/body justification. In this variation, inadequate performance is attributed to not being "in shape" or to not having the right "muscle tone." Athletes have trouble because they haven't had enough practice, or because they have over-practiced. And, of course, there is the quarterback whose throwing arm just never got on track. Then, too, there is the problem of being too keyed-up for the big event or, conversely, being too rested and relaxed, thereby losing that old "competitive edge."

Just as a professional can attribute a poor performance to fatigue or exhaustion, so too the average person can complain of a similar interference: "I haven't done that much today, but I'm mentally exhausted," or "I'm really dragging today; I haven't been able to sleep well for the last couple of nights." All these justifications which implicate a temporary or permanent bodily state are designed to convince any observers that they must judge our behavior according to a more lenient standard, one which acknowledges that you can't expect a strong performance from a weak body.

An even more subtle self/body distinction is frequently called into action. It is more subtle, because instead of treating mind and body as though they were different entities, it assumes that things in your head, such as thoughts and feelings, are uncontrollable bodily processes. Under this rationale, all kinds of thoughts or feelings, both good and bad, can supposedly interfere and cause inappropriate behavior. For example:

> "I've been so depressed lately that I just can't seem to do anything right."
>
> "I'm so worried about whether I'll get accepted to med-school that I can't concentrate on my courses."
>
> "I've been so happy since I got accepted to med-school that I can't concentrate on my courses."
>
> "I guess being in love will even make somebody like me behave foolishly."

## WHAT TIME IS IT?

Poor decisions, acts of incompetence, and general stupidity are often justified or explained away through the technique of associating them with a particular—and always bad—time of day. For example:

> "I just can't do anything when I first get up in the morning."
>
> "I can't function until I've had my second cup of coffee."
>
> "It takes me two or three hours to really get going in the morning."
>
> "I can never get anything done just before lunch."
>
> "I always feel drowsy right after lunch."
>
> "I always seem to run out of steam in the afternoon."
>
> "There's no way I can concentrate when it gets close to quitting time."
>
> "When I get home from work I'm always too exhausted to do anything."
>
> "I always need to just sit and relax right after dinner."
>
> "I find it impossible to concentrate at the end of a long day."
>
> "It's time to go to sleep. I can't make any decisions now."

The obvious conclusion to be drawn from these often-heard quotes? Anytime is bad.

And, of course, bad times don't have to be parts of days—they can be whole days. On Monday you're still recovering from the weekend. Tuesday, Wednesday, and Thursday just seem so long that you get into the mid-week doldrums, and then you're so grateful that it's Friday that you can't get anything done. And we all know you can't expect anything from a person on the weekend. As people like to say, "It's just one of those days."

Similarly, some people even attempt to justify their failings in terms of a whole season of the year: "I just hate spring/summer/fall/winter. The only time I really feel right, and feel like I can get it together is in spring/summer/fall/winter." Likewise holidays, birthdays, and other "special" times are used to excuse any number of personal excesses (too much to drink, too much to eat, sexual lapses, rowdy behavior, excessive spending).

Time also is employed as a social justification device in excuses explaining how long someone has been doing something. Failures usually are attributed to inexperience—the old "Hi-I'm-new-here" technique. After making an obvious error, people will say something like:

> "I've never done this sort of thing before."
> "This is only the second time I've ever tried this."
> "I've never used this recipe before."
> "It's only my first day/week/month on the job."

Or someone will drive into a gas station to ask directions, but invariably must explain, "I'm a stranger in these parts." And professional sports figures are especially prone to justifying a less than wonderful performance by explaining to Howard Cosell and the viewing audience, "Well, it's only my first year in the league. I'm just a rookie, and I have a lot of things to learn yet."

Of course, poor performance can also be socially justified in terms of having spent too much time at something:

> "I've been at this for twelve hours straight."

"I've done this so often that the edge is gone; I just can't seem to do it as well anymore."

"Doing the same thing day after day, you just start to slow down; it's inevitable."

Time also gets implicated in social justifications which involve age: "Well, you can't expect much from an old fogie like me. Remember, I'm just not as young as I used to be."

Time, of course, is *not* the problem. Rather it is a shorthand way of describing boredom, fatigue, ineptness, or just a general lack of knowledge.


## IF ONLY I HAD A. . .

Many behaviors involve the use of tools or implements. For example, almost all sporting activities involve equipment (balls, rackets, clubs, bats, and special playing surfaces), and some require special clothing and shoes. Likewise, cooks need stoves, utensils, pots and pans, and all the proper ingredients. Workers need tools, machines, pencils, and paper. Clearly, it is unreasonable to expect someone to live up to a general standard of performance unless he has the right implements.

Look at Stan, the tennis player. He has hit most of his shots into the net or out of bounds. As he and his opponent switch sides, he comments, "I just can't get used to this racket. Mine's being restrung, so I had to borrow my son's. And even though it is the same make and size and everything, it just doesn't have the same feel." Or maybe he left his Adidas at home and had to wear P. F. Flyers. Or maybe he forgot his sweat band today.

Then there's Bea, who didn't wash her hair this morning because she couldn't find the cord for her hairdryer.

And Ralph, whose souffle didn't turn out too well because he only had one egg. And Susan, who didn't get her term paper finished because she needed a new typewriter ribbon.

A whole world of mistakes can be justified away by blaming some implement, ingredient, piece of equipment, or lack thereof. Secretaries can't get used to the new typewriters. Home repairmen could do a better and quicker job if they had the right tools with them. People stumble because of new shoes. Singers can't perform properly because the microphone is strange or the lights are too bright. Physicians would have made the proper diagnosis if only they had had the proper equipment. Since almost all behaviors involve the use of some implement or object, these justifications are extremely common. Of course, if we are on the receiving end, these excuses can become very irritating, especially if we are paying for incomplete or inept services. It is tempting to cite the old aphorism, "It's a poor carpenter who blames his tools."

## THIS JUST ISN'T THE RIGHT PLACE

Television talk shows occasionally have animals as guests. At least once or twice a year some trainer will appear with her talking parrot, mynah bird, or robin redbreast. After a big build-up about how many languages the bird can speak, the camera and microphone are moved in to close range. And what happens? The trainer talks furiously, but the poor bird does exactly nothing. "It's the lights and all these people around. He talks like crazy at home, Merv. The studio is just the wrong place for him to talk; it makes him nervous." These birds hear these lines so often, it's a wonder they don't learn to give the explanations themselves.

The point of this story is, of course, that many social

justifications take the form of attributing inappropriate behavior to the fact that the person (or bird) just isn't in "the
right place." This right place could be another house,
office, city, or even another country, but always the justifier
could do better if only he were somewhere else. For example, "This room is just too crowded for me to think."
"There's something about Baltimore that makes me feel
exhausted." "My act works much better on the stage at the
Bijou."

A variation of this theme is the very familiar situation
in which we are stopped by an acquaintance who just has to
tell us (1) this hilarious story, (2) the exciting play in yesterday's ballgame, (3) the cute and remarkable thing little
Sally did yesterday, or (4) the rapier-like reply used to reduce to size some particularly offensive boor. The story or
incident is related. We listen, waiting in vain for a punch
line. Did that person just recite an incredibly dull story? No,
of course not. The problem is, "You had to be there."

### HOW'S THE WEATHER?

Neither wind, nor rain, nor sleet, nor balmy summer days
can deter the inveterate justifier:

> "I can't do anything with my hair in this kind of
> weather."
> "In this heat I'm worn out before I even get
> started."
> "The humidity is so high I can barely move, let
> alone get any work done."
> "Rainy days always get me down."
> "In this kind of cold weather my fingers seem to
> stay numb all the time."

"I find it impossible to concentrate on work on days as pretty as this."

The weather, of course, is just one of the many features of the general environment that supposedly can affect behavior. In addition to implicating the wind or the heat in excusing mistakes or poor performance, we like to blame almost any characteristic of the environment, whether something physical and real ("I tripped on that crack in the sidewalk") or totally ephemeral ("I'm having a run of bad luck" or "The gods seem to be against me").

An extreme form of this kind of social justification is regularly provided by astrology and astrologists. To astrology afficionados, action must be seen in terms of the workings of the stars; therefore, inappropriate behavior can be justified with statements such as, "My astrologer said that this would be a bad day for interpersonal relationships," or "Well, my chart did say that April would be a bad month for financial dealings," "I'm sorry for being so inconsiderate, but that's the way we Aquarians are."

By getting the observer to acknowledge an extenuating circumstance, we force him to use a lenient substandard which is consistent with our behavior. So whether it's the weather, the time of day, the place, the month, our weak eyes, our trick knee, or what someone else told us to do, one thing is obvious. I DIDN'T DO IT, SO DON'T BLAME ME!

# 7

# No One Understands Me

## *Switching Standards in Mid-Faux Pas*

Aside from pointing out extenuating circumstances which dictate that a sub-standard be applied to our behavior, there are two other general ways of working with standards to effect a justification. One involves agreeing with the relevance of a particular standard but asserting that it isn't very important or of any significant consequence. Another tack involves an attempt to get the observer to use an entirely different standard in judging our behavior. We'll begin by examining this latter one.

Most of us subscribe to a large number of values:

| | |
|---|---|
| pragmatism | idealism |
| generosity | thrift |
| self-confidence | humility |
| spirituality | materialism |
| individual freedom | equality |
| self-indulgence | self-control |
| commitment | open-mindedness |
| boldness | caution |
| national security | world peace |
| discretion | total honesty |
| assertiveness | modesty |

And when we publicly testify to our commitment to one of these values (e.g., individual freedom), we frequently talk as though we endorsed that value without qualification. However, when we move from the abstract level of discussion, which allows us merely to deal with the value in general terms, to the level at which we must actually implement the value, things become much more complicated. The complexity of most supposedly simple, everyday decisions (what to wear: "I like to be casual, but the boss wants me to wear a suit"; what to eat: "I know spinach will keep me healthy, but I'd rather eat a Hostess Twinkie"; who to invite to a party: "Jan is one of my best friends, but Sue can't stand her, and Sue is chairperson for the garden club I want to get into") results from conflicts between our many values. For example, while we strongly value freedom, we also value personal responsibility (i.e., "your-freedom-ends-at-the-tip-of-my-nose"). We value hard work *and* relaxation, rationality *and* emotionality, discipline *and* the right to self-indulgence. Balancing and integrating these conflicting values requires a great deal of time, energy, and mental anguish.

An additional complication is that by endorsing so many values, we leave ourselves open to a wide variety of possible attacks from others—and there always seems to be at least one person ready to mount an assault. It does not seem to matter how obviously "right" our position is: we may view it one way, and so may many others, but there is always someone who will disagree. This is the old "damned-if-you-do-damned-if-you-don't" syndrome. We value rationality, and when we make a hard, calculated decision, there will be someone to criticize us for being insensitive and unfeeling. When we assert our independence, someone will label us as "aloof." When we want the company of others, someone will chide us for being "too dependent." If we display our sentimentality, some sniper will call us "immature" and "unrealistic."

The one way out of this seemingly hopeless dilemma is—you guessed it—to justify. We do this by strongly asserting the value which guided our decision. For example, if we are criticized for being too suspicious, we point out that what with all the dangers lurking around us all the time, one *cannot be too suspicious*. Or we may acknowledge the other value, but without a pause go on to declare the overwhelming virtue of our position. Thus, if someone criticizes us for being too lenient on a child that has just been naughty, we may agree that "Yes, it *is* important that children be taught to respect their elders, but we must remember that to too severely react to what is a very natural display of youthful enthusiasm might be damaging to Little Johnny's psyche. Therefore I prefer not to discipline directly, but to teach by my own example." Likewise we are not "severe," but simply "firm"; we are not "inhibited," rather we are "self-controlled" or "cautious"; we are not "impulsive," we are "free spirited"; we are not "gullible," we are "trusting."

The gist of this approach to social justification is to respond when attacked for a deficiency in terms of one value by attempting to wrap ourselves in the flag-like blanket of a different—and sometimes opposite—value. When criticized for frivolously spending so much money for a pair of new shoes, a woman might straighten her shoulders with pride and begin a discourse on the many reasons why you just can't beat quality, and that if you want quality you have to pay a little more for it ("They're handmade, the very best of leathers, extremely comfortable to wear, and they last forever—besides they were reduced"). But in the next breath, this same person might describe a purchase she made later, on the way home, in which she stopped at the supermarket and picked up a couple of pairs of pantyhose ("They're just as comfortable as the more expensive ones, they look every bit as well—in fact, only the wearer can tell that they are not stockings by Dior—and besides, I always seem to get a run in them the first time I wear the expensive ones").

As suggested in this example—and in the one which follows—most of us are sufficiently versatile to be able to switch from acting as though we wholeheartedly endorse one value to acting as though our lives are dedicated to the very opposite one.

When a man is criticized for his blunt remarks regarding someone else's clothes, hairstyle, basic personality, way of life, etc., he may justify his comments by proclaiming another value: "Look, I was only being honest. That's something that happens to be very important to me, one of the basic tenets of the way I lead my life." A few days later this same man is accused by a friend of not having told the truth about that same friend's new puce velour gaucho pants (the friend having been the object of general public ridicule at a recent pool party). The man explained to his friend—with some indignation—that honesty is not necessarily the best policy, and that he had not spoken his true feelings about the puce velour gaucho pants because he did not want to hurt his friend's feelings: "Politeness and tact are among the important things to remember in life."

Through this tactic of switching allegiance from one value to another, we attempt to get our critic to judge our action according to the standards which correspond with this new value. Thus, in terms of the preceding example, the man was asserting that his less-than-completely-frank remark regarding his friend's attire should be judged in relation to standards concerning "tact" and the need to have "concern for the feelings of others," rather than in accordance with standards for honesty. Likewise, the decision to purchase expensive shoes should be judged in terms of standards stressing the importance of quality, while the decision to buy inexpensive stockings should be evaluated according to standards which stress expediency and convenience. Since most of us have so many values, and since we are committed to all of them, it is very easy to adopt this chameleon approach so that our actions blend with the expedient value—the one that makes us look most attractive at the moment.

Think of these conflicts in stated values in terms of a trial involving two very convincing and effective attorneys. The prosecution presents its case, carefully and rationally, arguing for the superiority of his side's value. The prosecution rests and we are convinced. But then it is the defense's turn, and she is equally effective in convincing us that the value that she is expounding is of the greatest possible merit. Once again, we are convinced. Each side has succeeded in rationally persuading us of the superiority of it's own value. But one has to wonder if "rational persuasion" is the real basis of these rituals, especially if one considers that the next day these same attorneys will be equally effective in defending or prosecuting exactly the opposite positions. Like good lawyers, we all need to be persuasive and adaptable. Indeed, most of us have had the experience of doing one thing, justifying its validity, and then subsequently doing something totally contradictory and likewise justifying its validity. Perhaps one of the following examples will have a familiar ring.

Many of us have had the experience of being in a neighborhood, realizing that a friend lived there, and deciding to "drop by" for a visit. Usually this friend will have said at some point, "When you're in the neighborhood, drop by." The strained smile which greets us spells polite hospitality, but fails in its attempt to belie pained disbelief. "We can't stay. We were just in the neighborhood and decided to stop by and say 'hello.' " And so we excuse ourselves. Then as we are about to get into our car, another friend—also of that neighborhood—happens by and says, "Why, you were going to leave without stopping in for a visit." To which we reply, "Well, we didn't want to impose. We would never drop by without warning you first."

The chances of these two events occurring in direct sequence are highly unlikely. The likelihood that the responses would be one and the other at different times *is* high, however. It is not a question of whether both responses are truth or lies—they are expedient, and they serve, for the moment, as effective justifications.

We also believe in sometimes asking for something "free," and if someone looks askance at us, we justify, "Well, there's no harm in trying." But don't we also sometimes insist on "paying our way," and not asking for handouts—"I have my pride. I won't allow myself to look cheap."

And we go out to dinner in a dress or coat-and-tie because we believe in looking "nice" in public, and out of a sense of decorum and respect for others, or because we want to avoid any interpersonal conflict. And we go out to dinner dressed in jeans and T-shirts, because we believe in "comfort" and that people should be freed from the restraints of society's bourgeois values.

It may be that at the moment we are sincerely convinced of the superiority of one value over another; or it may be that one value applies to some situations and that the opposite value applies to others. These two comments notwithstanding, it is hard to disagree with the critic who argues that people basically adopt whichever value suits their own interest at a particular time. But we are not concerned here with whether the critic—who argues that people hide their petty self-interests beneath a cover of grand values—is correct or not. Rather, we want simply to be aware of how it is possible to justify actions by trying to convince an observer to use a different set of values or standards in judging our behavior. And how, if we are not careful, we can get caught in the revolving door of our own pronounced values.

The other general approach to working with standards alluded to at the beginning of this chapter involves attempting to convince the observer that the standard we have just violated isn't really very important. Since how much this observer will disapprove of us is directly related to how important the standard is to him, we can potentially reduce the disapproval by getting him to decrease the importance he attaches to the standard. If this sounds simple, don't be fooled—it is usually quite difficult to pull off.

This approach to social justification can be illustrated with the case of a college student who must report his semester's grades to his parents. Suppose he had a fairly good semester, three A's and one B, but he did get a C too. His parents are paying a great deal of money for their son's tuition, and they, in turn, expect all A's and B's. So immediately upon giving the report to his parents, he points out that the course he got the C in is not his major. It was only an elective and not even a required course. In terms of social justification, the thrust of his comment is that it isn't *important* whether or not he gets a C in a course that isn't itself essential. Of course, he could have justified the whole thing by implicating the teacher ("He was such a dull and stupid lecturer") or by emphasizing time ("That class met at eight in the morning"), but instead he tried to decrease the importance his parents associate with the standard of (consistently) getting high grades. If it had been a bad semester (all C's), he might have tried to convince his parents that the really important things to be gained from "the college experience" were acquired outside the classroom—and not surprisingly, he's been "experiencing" a whole lot—and therefore grades aren't really that important.

Conflicts between different generations frequently produce social justifications which attack the importance of standards. Members of the "older generation" seem to be constantly judging the conduct of young people according to standards which these young people do not consider important or even any longer valid. Typically in these conflicts, members of the younger generation make such statements as:

> "But Mom, that just doesn't matter anymore."
> "Those concepts have no relevance in today's world."
> "Don't you realize that the times have changed?"
> "Daddy, don't be so old-fashioned!"
> "But *everybody* does it now."

Members of the older generation seldom find these assertions persuasive, but eventually they do decrease the importance they give to certain standards simply because their children persist in violating them.

People generally prefer to associate with others who place importance on the same standards. It is much easier that way because the use of justifications based on the importance of standards often produces heated verbal exchanges (fights). Also there is the pain of constantly being judged negatively for violating what one considers to be outmoded or unimportant standards, plus the effort of continually having to justify one's actions—it just becomes too much of a hassle. If these conflicts over standards cannot be resolved, the relationship probably will be terminated, or contact will at least be reduced to a bare minimum.

At times, two people may openly bargain and reach a mutual agreement by which both decrease the stated importance of some of their standards. This is most common in marriage situations in which *each* partner seems to constantly violate a standard that is important to the other. In order to avoid the constant conflict, anger, criticism, recriminations, and the need to justify, they may ultimately sign a bilateral disarmament treaty (''I'll quit complaining about your smoking if you'll quit telling me to hang up my clothes'') by agreeing to decrease the importance they give to certain standards.

The ''crisis situation'' provides another example of justifications based on decreasing the importance of standards. For example, a motorist is stopped for speeding. When the police officer approaches the car, the motorist says, ''Officer, I know I was exceeding the speed limit, but my wife is going to have a baby, and I was just hurrying home to take her to the hospital.''

The ''crisis situation'' may involve physical illness, severe mental depression, the loss of a loved one, marital separation, a personal financial crisis, or the loss of the pet gerbil. In these crisis situations we are frequently asked to decrease the importance we attach to a wide variety of everyday standards. As a result, we may not criticize people who are in the midst of such a crisis, even though they may look very unkempt, act very withdrawn, or even openly express a lot of anger and hostility. (Not surprisingly, some people attempt to take advantage of this tolerance by making life one crisis after another.) In order to avoid opening a Pandora's box of connected issues, suffice it to say the "crisis" justification is, in almost all cases, accepted as "honest"; it is the justifier alone who knows where "honesty" ends and the calculated manipulation of the emotions of others takes over.

So whether it's a question of different values, or one of changing the importance of standards, the goal is the same: "I am justified in what I do, and if you don't agree, then you simply don't understand."

# 8

# Yes, that's True, But. . .

*Justifying the Total Self*

There are times when there is just no way to make one of our errant actions seem permissible or even minimally excusable. In these cases no amount of effort to work with standards or with the observer's perception of our behavior will be sufficient to justify away some negligent actions. In these instances, we are faced with the fact that we have committed an unjustifiable act, and fear as a consequence that the other person may allow this single slip-up to color his overall impression of us.

In these situations, we must forego any attempt to justify the specific inappropriate behavior, and instead switch tactics and justify our *whole* self. We admit the one mistake, but try to represent ourselves as basically worthwhile.

In order to do this we must introduce additional (favorable) information about ourselves, thereby attempting to prevent the observer from basing his overall judgment of us on our one indiscrete act. The general idea of this approach is, "Yes I admit that was a bad thing to do, but remember, I do have these other good qualities. And of course, it will never happen again. Scout's honor."

## I'M SORRY

In Kurt Vonnegut's novel, *God Bless You, Mr. Rosewater*, Fred Rosewater tells his wife, "Other people say, 'Hello' or 'Goodbye!' We always say, 'Excuse me,' no matter what we're doing." And so we do. Most of us offer a couple of dozen apologies a day and some people offer a dozen dozen. The two most popular are "I'm sorry" and "excuse me," which serve as social justifications by conveying several implicit but clear messages.

By apologizing we more or less condemn our own behavior. But the fact that we publicly admit our errant act indicates one of our good qualities—honesty. Our apology shows that we are not sneaky, devious, or the kind of person who covers up inappropriate, illegal, or immoral acts. The message is, "At least I'm big enough to admit my mistakes."

The second important message is that we do know what the appropriate form of a particular behavior is. In essence we're saying, "Yes I did that dumb thing, but at least I know what's right, and that should count for something." We try to convince the observer that our knowledge of the right way to behave is another good point in our favor.

Another message implicit in an apology is the promise that we will not behave inappropriately *in the future*. This message is based on the following subtle logic:

1. "You can see that I condemn myself for behaving inappropriately and that condemnation is painful,"
2. "I'm not the kind of person who likes pain," therefore
3. "I will behave appropriately in the future because I want to avoid this kind of pain."

The message is, "In the future you can count on me to do the right thing and that's yet another good quality I have."

An additional point in our favor is that by condemning our own action we relieve the observer of the onerous task of condemning us. By apologizing, we free the other person from the necessity of denouncing us, clearing the way for a graceful "Well, okay. But don't let it happen again."

By impuning our own action we also communicate that we sincerely believe in the validity of the violated standard. Our *sincerity* is attested to by the fact that we are willing to condemn ourselves as well as others who violate the standard. In a sense, the fact that we condemn ourselves rather than waiting for the censure of others further supports our sincerity. In other words, when we step on someone's toes, our subsequent apology indicates that yes, while our foot was in the wrong place, at least our heart is in the right one.

The idea that "love means never having to say you're sorry" is easily understood in terms of social justification. Idealistically, if someone loves us, he or she will always love us, and never dislike us because of those things we do. If our lover won't dislike us, then there is no need to say "I'm sorry" or to offer any kind of justification.

In everyday social relationships an apology is not a very powerful tool. The weakness of an apology is that it will work well only after minor blunders. We can anticipate its success only when we are certain the offended person will not think we intended the negligent action.

For example, no one would think we intended to jostle

a stranger in an elevator, to step on someone's foot in a theater, or to purposely let a door swing closed on the person behind us. Similarly, our friends are unlikely to think we intended to disturb their meal by reaching across their plate to get the salt, or that we meant to harrass them by not responding immediately to their request for the butter dish. A simple apology will suffice in these situations: the inappropriate behavior is neither intended, nor is it very bad.

If there is a chance, however, that our behavior will be perceived as deliberate, and therefore extremely inappropriate, then an apology won't suffice. For example, in a disorganized line at a supermarket, a patron may inadvertently begin to edge his shopping cart ahead of another customer who has seniority in the line. The patron will not only apologize, but will add another social justification such as, "I didn't realize that you were in this line," or "I wasn't even watching what I was doing." The actual inappropriate behavior is relatively minor, especially since the patron quickly retracts his cart. However, it is certainly possible that the offended customer might think the patron intended to sneak into the line. After all, there are a lot of pushy people in the world, especially in supermarkets. Because the inappropriate behavior could be interpreted as deliberate, the patron must add another social justification to his apology.

When we offer an apology, we sometimes explicitly say we won't repeat the inappropriate behavior in the future. A husband mentions something undesirable about his wife's family, and she explodes in anger. The husband replies, "Look, I'm sorry. I'll never mention your mother's many faults again." By promising not to repeat the inappropriate behavior, we point out that we are still worthwhile persons. We try to regain acceptance by conveying the idea that we aren't really so bad, since we will do the appropriate thing from now on.

## IF AT FIRST YOU DON'T SUCCEED...

A variation on the technique of promising to improve in the future is to immediately repeat the behavior, but doing it correctly this next time. This obviously has the advantage of demonstrating our good intentions. Occasionally a pianist will begin a piece, then stop, and after a nine-second pause, begin the work again. Similarly, a student may get off to a bad start on an oral report and then abruptly stop and say, "Let me just begin that whole thing again." Mr. Mnemonic, ever the memory expert, realizes that he just called William by the wrong name. To guarantee that William knows that he really does know the right name, he quickly introduces two or three "William's" into the conversation, and maybe even one or two "Bill's."

This technique of repeating the behavior is especially common in conversation when we mispronounce a word or use the wrong word, such as an antonym. We often say up when we meant down, right when we meant left, and increase for decrease. Typically people know what we meant, but we're careful to guard our social standing anyway. ("Oh, did I say 'old.' I'm sorry, you know I meant 'young!' ")


## BUT I AM A GREAT...

The garbage disposal is stuck and Bill attempts to free it with a broom handle, which only creates more damage. He looks up and sees his wife, June, frowning and shaking her head. He says, "I may not be much of a plumber, but I have a good job of my own and can afford to pay somebody else to fix it. So there."

Switching to the offensive, Bill complains, "Anyway,

the reason this thing got stuck in the first place is that you let the garbage accumulate and put it all down in there at once.''

June is prepared for this criticism and replies, ''Look, I never said I was a great maid, but you have to admit that I am a darn good cook.''

Both members of this congenial couple are using the technique of explicitly pointing out their achievements in other areas of life. Bill doesn't try to justify his blundering with the broom, but instead mentions the irrelevant fact that he has a good job. Although June just overloaded the disposal, she talks about her success as a cook. The only thing that makes these irrelevant facts about other accomplishments vaguely relevant to the present situation is that they counter the negative implications of the blunders.

This technique of pointing out our good qualities to counter our mistakes is an extremely common form of social justification. A student who just flunked a math test talks about her achievements in her history course. The secretary who just forgot an important telephone message changes the topic to the efficiency with which a typing assignment was completed. A university professor who just lectured an entire class to sleep tells his colleague about a recently successful research project, while one who hasn't published any research in five years talks enthusiastically about his innovative new class.

## Oops!

One of the ways to counter the negative effects of mistakes is to immediately own up to them. So, after spilling some coffee, we say ''Oh, oh,'' or after we have dropped a utensil, we exclaim ''Oops!'' In writing a letter we insert "(sp?)" after words which we sense are misspelled. When a guest politely indicates that she requested her coffee "black," the host, who has just served it with milk and sugar, exclaims, "Now why did I do a dumb thing like that." A driver who just missed a freeway exit shakes her head and tells a passenger, "I knew I'd miss it." After making a cruel remark during an argument, we might comment, "I don't know why I said that. I didn't mean to." By admitting our error, we indicate that it wasn't intended and that we didn't know it would happen. Our goal is to mitigate the negative implications of our blunder by willingly admitting the error, forestalling censure through the admission that it was an inappropriate (and clumsy/stupid/inconsiderate/etc.) thing to have done.

### I'M SO EMBARRASSED!

Moments of strong personal embarrassment produce feelings of pain, anxiety, and discomfort. Even the memory of them haunts us. In fact, embarrassment is such an unpleasant experience that most of us don't even like to think about it. When we do think about it, we usually consider embarrassment to be the consequence of something gone wrong—the emotional end product of our social errors and blunders. From the perspective of social justification, however, embarrassment is not an end in itself, but is instead a means to an end. As with other justifications, it has the effect of minimizing the negative impressions created by our inappropriate behavior.

Embarrassment has not been systematically researched, but it seems to occur most frequently during early adolescence, and to be slightly more common among females than males. Children do not seem to display embarrassment until the age of two, and almost all of them seem to be capable of it by age four. Thus it seems that embarrassment is learned during these two years. And while it is not precisely known how children learn to become embarrassed, a simple conditioning process seems to be involved. For example, Little Tommy is caught with his hand in the cookie jar or in his own underpants. Since Tommy has learned that Mommy doesn't like such actions, his blood pressure rises as he braces himself in anticipation of punishment. But Mommy interprets his red face as a sign of embarrassment, so instead of a spanking or a scolding, Tommy gets a loving "Why, Tommy, you're embarrassed! How cute!" Little Tommy is relieved that he didn't get spanked, but he has no idea that his increased heart rate changed the color in his face or that his mother interpreted this as a sign of early moral development. But Little Tommy is on the road to learning to be "red faced" when caught in the act of behaving inappropriately.

When doting parents and grandparents affectionately say, "How cute! She's embarrassed!" children quickly learn that being embarrassed is socially acceptable and in fact is a way to garner praise. During late adolescence, however, embarrassment produces reactions such as "Why are you embarrassed over something like that?" or "Grow up. You shouldn't be embarrassed." At this age, embarrassment is more likely to be criticized than to be praised. The teenager's slightly older peers treat it as a lack of both sophistication and maturity, and as a result, embarrassment occurs less frequently. Some people continue to experience frequent blushes of embarrassment into young adulthood, but for most of us it becomes less common. In sum, embarrassment is a response appropriate to certain ages and situations, and how often it occurs is largely determined by whether or not it is praised or disapproved.

The idea that our embarrassment is controlled by other people, that it is learned, and has utility as a means to an end may seem surprising. On closer inspection, however, it is clear that embarrassment conveys a considerable amount of information. The act of being embarrassed communicates to observers the same kind of messages as does an apology.

The fact that we are embarrassed indicates that we recognize that we did something wrong and, by implication, that we know the proper way to behave. By becoming embarrassed, we admit our errant action, condemn ourselves, and indicate regret that we committed the action. By condemning ourselves, we relieve the observer of the burden of doing it for us. Finally, by becoming embarrassed, we implicitly promise that we will not again commit the inappropriate behavior. This promise is implied by the fact that while we get embarrassed, we don't run away from the situation, but stay and continue to participate. Only if we had really "blown it" would we turn and slink away.

The act of showing embarrassment is a legitimate form of social justification, an appropriate behavior following a misdeed. By becoming embarrassed, we indicate to onlookers that we do have many good qualities which should be considered and weighed against our mistake. The effectiveness of embarrassment as a social justification is reflected in the reaction we get from people if we don't get embarrassed following a major blunder as opposed to the way they react if we do get embarrassed. Generally to not show embarrassment is socially unacceptable and leaves us open to such criticisms as: "Has she no shame!"; "How could he! And not even a hint of embarrassment!"; or, "Have you no remorse?!" By being embarrassed we protect ourselves from such condemning remarks, thereby avoiding the fate of the social outcast. In fact, when we show embarrassment, people not only stop criticizing (and disliking) us, they go so far as to step in and console us. They say things like, "That's okay, don't worry about it," and "Oh, that could happen to anyone." Then they pat us on the back and talk real fast to be sure that we're not too upset.

Embarrassment typically occurs when our actions are inconsistent with our stated values. For example, if we profess modesty, but our action reflects vanity, we are likely to get embarrassed. If we claim to want a platonic relationship, and an action reveals our secret sexual desires, we will become embarrassed. If we preach honesty, but get caught cheating, embarrassment will surely result. Therefore, we are most likely to become embarrassed in situations in which:

1. There is a clear standard which we claim to endorse.
2. Our action is completely inconsistent with this standard.
3. The observer knows we endorse the standard and that our behavior is clearly inconsistent.
4. We know the observer will disapprove of our inconsistency.
5. There is no alternate way available to justify the behavior.

Thus, embarrassment is essentially a social justification of last resort, employed on those occasions when we have behaved in a manner blatantly inconsistent with our professed values. If we didn't need to continue the relationship with the other person, we might just leave the scene of our crime. But, since we can't flee, the only social justification left to us is the humbling act of embarrassment.

This concept of embarrassment as a social justification of last resort can be illustrated by considering what it is like to do something utterly inconsistent with one of our most important declared values. We have a few values which we consider of paramount importance (e.g., honesty, sexual fidelity, concern for others, loyalty) and to which we frequently—and publicly—pledge allegiance. Since we have declared ourselves publicly ("Well, you certainly would never catch me doing. . ."), when subsequently we *are* caught doing just that, there is very little we can say. The only thing we can do—short of suicide—is to let the world know just how "ashamed" we are, and how "guilty" we feel, by showing everyone that we are really and truly embarrassed. Please note that those values we hold most dear are also the potential sources of our greatest pain and embarrassment. Please note also that "shame" and "guilt"— and even the thorny question of "morality"—have nothing to do with embarrassment. The whole thing boils down to the simple violation of a standard and our reaction to getting caught. That reaction is only one thing—embarrassment.

The fact that people sometimes profess embarrassment for the blunders of others (e.g., parents for their children, one spouse for another, fans for a favorite athlete) does not contradict the idea that embarrassment functions as a form of social justification. Close analysis reveals that we typically get embarrassed only for those others who have some connection or relationship with us. In a sense, their errors might be viewed as a negative reflection on us (e.g., "How can you live with someone like that?"; "How can you be friends with her?"), which forces us to justify someone else's behavior as if it were our own. Thus our embarrassment is as much, if not more, for ourselves than it is for the other person. And for some people, embarrassment is such a strongly learned response that any linkage between themselves and a blunder, or even the memory of one, may be sufficient to produce a full emotional reaction.

And so to review, if we can't justify our misdeed in one of the standard and non-incriminating ways, we often must switch to a demonstration of our general worth as a person. We do this by pointing out—as subtly as possible—that we do have good qualities, as demonstrated by our acts of apology, our promise to improve and to mend our errant ways, our sincere and honest acknowledgements of error, and our obvious embarrassment.

# 9

# A Case of Temporary Unreality

*The Process of Mystification*

A man at a cocktail party makes a suggestive remark to a woman he knows only casually. When her response is less than encouraging—in fact, she staggers back in undisguised fear and loathing—he quickly counters with, "No, no, I was only kidding."

At the church "pot-luck supper," Mary says to Sally, "Whoever made the chipped beef was a little heavy with the Elmer's Glue." Immediately realizing from her shocked expression that Sally was the chef in question, Mary hastens to cover her gaff by saying, "I'm only teasing, of course. It's delicious. Would you write down the recipe for me?"

In both of these situations, the person justifying is using an interesting variation of the re-definition technique. In its most extreme form, this approach involves treating our actions as though they were not real. We accept the fact that the behavior did occur and that, yes, we did it, but we act as though the whole thing was a fantasy, certainly in no way representative of our true selves. And so, just as a criminal may plead temporary insanity to excuse an illegal action, we sometimes justify our errant actions with a plea of "temporary unreality."

This technique of arguing temporary unreality is demonstrated when we try to say we were "just joking," "only kidding," or "merely teasing." And it is normally used only when the other person is obviously offended or shocked by our behavior. For example, a husband hears of a "wife-swapping" club in the neighborhood. He doesn't want to admit that he finds the idea somewhat appealing, at least not without first finding out his wife's opinion on the matter. So he offhandedly—and somewhat cautiously—says after dinner one evening, "Instead of bridge tonight with the Joneses, why don't we just swap bed partners. It'd beat a small slam any day." When his wife, who had heard of the neighborhood antics and who had not been at all titillated by the idea, stares at him aghast, he quickly covers himself by saying, "Why, you should see your face, Dear. I was only joking. You should know that I only have eyes for you, Honey."

And so, what was a quick peek at someone's secret desires, even more quickly becomes "only a joke." From experience, most of us know that there are many statements which become "jokes" when we realize that the other person (the object of the joke) becomes offended or angry. It is this common knowledge that makes jokes and teases the vehicles of small elements of truth.

A more subtle version of this technique of treating our actions as though they were not real is represented by what is commonly known as "nervous laughter." Almost all of us employ this technique, using a laugh that may last for several seconds ("tee-hee-hee-hee") or may be only a short cluck ("tee"). Nervous laughter serves as a social justification device in essentially the same way as does the statement, "I was only kidding." What the nervous laugh indicates is that we didn't really mean what we just said, or that our behavior was in jest and therefore needn't be taken seriously. The logic behind this is that if the behavior wasn't real, then its appropriateness or inappropriateness can't be judged in terms of the standards applied to normal, everyday behavior. Thus by laughing—and thereby defining an action as "unreal"—we effectively remove it from the realm of behaviors that can be used as a basis for judging our worth as persons.

You've probably noticed that during interviews on television talk shows or in studio news programs—usually with such dignitaries as Henry Kissinger or Henry Winkler—the interviewer will sometimes give a little nervous laugh after asking a very personal or revealing question. The distinguished interviewee may very well not want to answer the question, and in fact may find it rude to the point of insult, but he probably won't. The interviewer has covered himself—his little nervous laugh indicated that he wasn't really serious in asking the question (although chances are he wouldn't have minded if the guest had answered), and therefore he should not be considered to be pushy, tactless, or rude. Nor was the question or his behavior inappropriate—it was "only a joke, tee, hee."

Nervous laughter frequently is used *before* the other people present have had an opportunity to respond to our action. This suggests that when we emit a nervous laugh, we have anticipated that the other person probably will disapprove of what we are going to do or say. This observation implies that nervous laughter is most likely to occur when we think our behavior is going to infringe on the other person's rights or contradict his attitudes and thereby create substantial disapproval. Some examples which exemplify this process should help to clarify this phenomenon.

Nervous laughter is especially common when we are going to express a novel idea or an attitude which may well contradict another person's ideas or attitudes. For example, in discussing a business decision made by his boss, an employee may say—when talking to that boss—"Well, maybe we should have just done the opposite, tee-hee, and then maybe none of this would have happened, chuckle-chortle." If the boss then indicates that in fact he did make the right decision and that the error lay in its execution, then the underling has, so to speak, "covered his ass" by allowing his boss to interpret his remark as a sort of ironic aside, or at the very least something said in jest. On the other hand, if the boss grimly agrees that his decision was less than sterling, then the employee implicitly takes credit—and hopefully wins Brownie points—for pointing out the error in judgment.

Nervous laughter is also frequently employed to qualify our statement when we criticize someone. For example, a woman may say to a man she is dating, "Hee-hee, don't you think that bathing suit is a little (chortle) revealing (chuckle) to wear in front of my parents?"

Generally speaking, since nervous laughter typically occurs only when we anticipate that the other person may rebuke us for our comment, we would not then need to employ it when criticizing someone who is inferior to us in age, education, or professional standing. Superiors supposedly have the right to criticize their inferiors, and the inferiors supposedly have to take it. Thus the superiors don't anticipate being rebuked for their critical remarks, and therefore usually don't bother to justify by attaching the nervous laugh to the criticism. The person in the inferior position, however, the employee in the example above, will generally justify with nervous laughter. A more common example would be one in which the relations between a group of people had always involved formal appellations, such as Mr., Mrs., etc., with the superiors in the relationship freely addressing everyone by their first names, while the inferiors exercise continual caution in initiating any move toward an expression of more informal relations. Imagine the head of a company, Mr. William J. Grim, inviting a rising young executive, Mr. James Comer, to his home for dinner. Mr. Grim can easily start calling Jim Jim, but the first time Jim calls Mr. Grim "Bill" he will laugh nervously, especially if this might be interpreted as being just a little forward, and if Mr. Grim has not yet indicated the permissibility of informality ("Just call me Willie").

Most of us have had more than enough experience with the overly "friendly" and ingratiating salesperson. Before starting their actual sales pitch, such people usually try to establish a bond of commonality and mutual agreement with the customer. They do this by describing their own attitudes and interests as being in total agreement with the customer's ("Nice day, isn't it? Couldn't agree with you more"). Supposedly if they can establish a bond of similarity, they will gain the customer's trust. On the other hand, if they express attitudes in contradiction to those of the customer, they will be regarded with suspicion and will find it impossible to sell that incredible used car, insurance policy, or set of cookware. In this process of establishing similarity of attitudes and beliefs, salespeople often express an opinion and then give a nervous chuckle, usually of the intolerably hearty variety. If the customer indicates agreement, then the salesperson typically will reaffirm the opinion by restating it. Thus:

*Salesperson:*   Looks as though the President is up to his neck in trouble (*laughter*).
*Customer:*   Yeah, you said it.
*Salesperson:*   Yeah, he's really made a mess of it.

However, if the customer does not agree with the salesperson's statement, then there was that laugh which indicated that it was all a joke anyway. Thus:

*Salesperson:*   Looks as though the President is up to his neck in trouble (*laughter*).
*Customer:*   I don't think he's in trouble. In fact, I think he's doing a fine job.
*Salesperson:*   (*Laughing*) Yeah, people criticize him a lot, but he's working all the time to improve things.

Of course, salespersons aren't the only ones who use nervous laughter to justify remarks, especially when the topic concerns politics, religion, sex, or some other delicate subject. We all do it, using it in much the same way as do politicians who have their aides issue "trial balloons." If the balloon floats and there is no public outcry for a beheading, then the politician will come out and publicly endorse the issue. If the balloon is shot down, however, the politician "just can't understand why his aide would have made such an unauthorized statement." (Tee-hee.) In much the same way, if our statements aren't immediately criticized, we drop the laugh and reindorse our position.

Another type of situation in which we frequently employ the nervous laugh is one in which we make a demand of someone and we're not sure how the other person will react (i.e., with compliance or a snort of irritation). For example, a woman says something about herself that is personally a bit more revealing than she had intended, and in an effort to not give it too much weight while at the same time begging her friend to keep her mouth shut, she will say in a mock-demanding tone, "Now shhhh, don't you dare repeat that," followed by a little nervous laugh. Likewise, a cafeteria patron is disappointed at the small portion of mystery meat he has been given. So he asks the employee behind the steam counter if he might have a slightly larger serving, and then he gives a nervous chortle. Similarly, a woman asks for postage stamps, and upon seeing that the clerk is going to give her those plain old everyday ones, she asks if she could have some of those "pretty ones" and then laughs (nervously).

We encounter dozens of examples of nervous-laughter situations every day. Suffice it to say, however, that while it may be used as a device for social justification for almost any inappropriate behavior, it seems to occur most frequently when we engage in an action which we definitely anticipate will be disagreeable to those around us. There are those people, however, who seem to add a nervous laugh as a postscript to almost everything they say and do. These people always seem to be tense, nervous, and/or frightened. They seem to anticipate that their every action will be objected to and criticized and, as a result, they constantly engage in nervous laughter in an unending effort to disassociate themselves from their behavior. Life is clearly unpleasant for these people. First, they have the belief that they are constantly being scrutinized and found wanting. Second, while most of us only use the nervous laugh to indicate our temporary unreality, these people seem to live lives of permanent unreality. They are always treating their actions as unreal and not really representative of themselves. But if they are not their behavior, then who are they? Whoever, they *are* annoying, but also evoke pity as well as condemnation.

Just as we sometimes laugh nervously before expressing an opinion, we also sometimes offer our verbal social justifications before actually engaging in an action. As with laughter, we give these pre-justifications when we anticipate that our behavior may be judged to be inappropriate. Essentially what we are doing when we pre-justify is warning the other people that we are about to do something that they may find inappropriate.

One way to do this is simply to request the other person to grant us permission to behave inappropriately. If brash Bill just goes ahead and asks a very personal question of a virtual stranger, he probably will be judged as living up to his reputation. But, if Bill says, "May I ask you a very personal question?" and gets permission ahead of time, then he can proceed with relative immunity. When we give Bill permission to engage in potentially inappropriate behavior, Bill cannot be held totally responsible for his actions, and we can no longer pass judgment on Bill's character on the basis of his otherwise pushy, forward, and thoroughly reprehensible behavior. In a sense, when we grant Bill's request, we take responsibility for his behavior.

Requests for permission to behave inappropriately—and therefore to be free of negative judgments—are extremely common. We all hear and/or make requests such as: "Can I ask you a favor?" "Do you mind if I let my hair down?" "Will you hold, please?" "Would you mind if I smoked a cigarette?" "May I call you by your first name?" and the most puzzling one of all, "May I speak honestly?" Does that mean everything up to this point has been a lie?

Under most circumstances we do our own social justifying. There are times when other people do our social justifying for us. These acts of assistance are generally carried out by loved ones and relatives. For example, at a dinner party the conversation drifts to the topic of a highly publicized pornographic movie. One lone individual indicates that he has seen the movie (and he doesn't offer any redeeming explanation). As most of the other guests pull back from him in an open display of repugnance and hostility, the lone man's wife rushes to his defense. "Oh I agree, the film is terrible. The only reason John went to see it was in connection with some research he was doing for the University." Maybe John didn't care whether other people approved or not. It didn't matter—his wife justified his actions for him.

Occasionally the person who has passed the negative judgment will actually provide the justification for the individual who behaved inappropriately. The following scene was observed in a grocery check-out line. A young male cashier charged a woman 89¢ for a can of frozen juice. The woman complained that the price is only 69¢. The boy picked up the can, looked at the price, and said, "Yeah, you're right." The woman then said, to the boy and to anyone else who might listen, "Sometimes the ink gets so smeared that it is impossible to tell exactly what the marked price is." In these instances in which our judge turns into our defender, the primary function of the justification the other person offers is to indicate that there are no hard feelings. That is, by justifying for the clerk, the customer indicates that she has not passed a negative judgment on him because of his inappropriate action. These justifications serve as an assurance that we are still in the other person's good graces.

Parents frequently justify for their children, especially if the children are relatively young. Children often spill food, knock things over, and make inopportune statements. When these things happen in front of other adults, the parents of these children will take care of the justifying. Little Heather's family goes to visit the home of friends; coffee is served and a special plate of cookies and a glass of milk are given to Little Heather. She spills the milk, complains that the cookies taste funny, and when admonished by her mother, she whines that she'd rather be at home than at this "stupid house." By this time, Dear Little Heather will be donning her mittens while her distraught parents frantically explain that The Dear missed her nap today and is tired, or that she always acts strange when she is in a new situation, or that the doctor says she is just at that age in which all children act negatively.

As may be apparent, when an individual socially justifies for another person, it is usually the case that the individual is justifying for himself rather than for the other person. One person's inappropriate behavior can have implications for the character and desirability of that person *and* for the character of the other individuals with whom he is linked. This "guilt-by-association" is readily apparent when a dog owner justifies the dog's incessant barking or unfortunate habits to an offended neighbor. A child is often viewed as a psychological extension of its parents to the extent that if a child misbehaves, many parents feel that it reflects negatively on them as good parents. Thus, when a mother socially justifies for her child, she could be trying to avoid the possibility that she will be judged as inadequate or inept as a mother. In a similar way, when a husband justifies for his wife, he could well be defending his definition of himself as capable of choosing a good—and unoffensive—person as a spouse. But one should be careful about apologizing or justifying for the actions of another, no matter what the relationship. If the person who engaged in the supposedly inappropriate behavior is neither apologetic nor intimidated, a justification of these actions might produce considerable resentment, and perhaps even put a severe strain on the relationship. Nonrepentant dogs have been known to bite their masters.

# 10

## But What Can You Expect from Someone with All My Problems?

*Chronic Justifications*

Wouldn't it be nice to have some magic device which would automatically justify all our inappropriate actions? Perhaps a little card or badge we could show to other people which would automatically erase their disapproval of any of our misdeeds? With our special badge we could operate with the ease of a James Bond or a special government agent, always justified in our actions. We wouldn't need to worry about whether we were going to misbehave or offend someone. We'd know that all we would have to do is flash our badge and people would say, "Oh, okay. I understand." We wouldn't have to worry over thinking up some new and clever justification to extract ourselves from our latest blunder. We would have the freedom to do just about anything we wanted. As soon as we committed a social offense, we could just flash our badge, and we'd get off without any questions, and without the need for further excuses.

Such a device exists. In fact, there are several of them, but they are not free. Indeed, the major drawback is that they come with a very high price tag, and the price is paid in terms of general social acceptability. The person who uses one of these badges must be resigned to a position of diminshed desirability, a lowered social standing. But once the terms have been accepted, a badge holder can still proceed without many additional restrictions, carrying out almost all the actions of normal persons. In fact, the badge holder has the freedom to do a lot of nasty, insulting, and inconsiderate things denied to "normal" persons. When someone criticizes a badge holder, a mere flash of the badge automatically excuses him or her from punishment. Before running out and buying one of these badges for our very own, however, we should examine some of the different ones available to us.


## ALCOHOLICS

The view has developed in our society that the fact that an individual is an alcoholic *explains* why he behaves as he does. Alcoholism frequently causes people to do many inappropriate things. Alcoholics have a reputation for missing work, for hurting themselves and/or others, for wasting money, lying, being generally irresponsible, for saying rude and unkind things, and for creating scenes. But since these types of inappropriate behavior supposedly result directly from the disease, the person who accepts the badge of an alcoholic acquires an all-purpose social justification. Anytime alcoholic badge holders do something inappropriate, they just show the offended person their badge, "I'm an Alcoholic. What can you expect?" As long as the alcoholics' behavior isn't disastrously offensive most people will continue to tolerate being around them, will invite them to parties, and will keep them on the payroll.

The badge of alcoholism does have its social price, but these costs aren't necessarily very great. Alcoholics will be viewed with suspicion by new acquaintances, and even old friends will not treat them with the same regard as they do non-alcoholics. On the whole, however, most people will just wink and say, "Well, maybe he does have a drinking problem, but he's really not that bad a guy." The alcoholic badge holders trade this slightly lowered social standing for a license to violate standards, and instead of condemnation, they receive virtually automatic exoneration, pity, and concern. And while there are many reasons why a person may become an alcoholic, one of the things that makes it easy to remain one is this license and its many extended benefits.

Alcoholic badge holders get several additional social advantages. Because people expect alcoholics to be irresponsible and act inappropriately, they try not to put them in situations in which they will have to be counted on to act responsibly. For example, Walt and Jean are getting ready to hold a party. Since Jean can't be relied on to help with any of the chores, Walt does them all. Jean just lounges around, slowly sipping a gin and tonic. The fact that Jean didn't help with the work doesn't stop her from attending the party, having a good time, or from receiving the expressions of gratitude from departing guests. Usually the alcoholic enjoys the benefits of the efforts of associates, but doesn't have to assume either the responsibilities or work.

Another distinct advantage to claiming the badge of alcoholism is that other people will do a great deal of our social justifying for us. And after all, it is quite easy, especially since they get to always use the same justification. If Jean makes an insulting remark to one of the party guests, Walt will ease over to the guest and quietly whisper, "Please forgive Jean. She has a bit of a drinking problem." And Jean goes her merry way, never having to personally show her badge.

This analysis of the alcoholic has been framed solely in terms of the orientation of social justification. It is not intended, of course, to deny medical, social, and psychological analyses of the benefits or costs of being an alcoholic.

The advantages the alcoholic badge wearer obtains, which are essentially the same for all badges, are as follows:

1.   An automatic and all-purpose social justification
2.   The freedom to be as irreverent and inconsiderate as desired
3.   Exclusion from a lot of work and responsibilities, but with permission to enjoy the fruits of others' efforts
4.   The assistance of others in providing justifications

The primary social cost of wearing this badge is being defined as lower in desirability than a non-alcoholic. The badge wearers are still socially acceptable to most people; it's just that they aren't perceived as quite up to par ("Sure Jean drinks a little too much, but she's still basically a nice person"). (It must be remembered, of course, that the family of the alcoholic experiences only the costs of the badge, and none of the benefits.)

The badge of alcoholism isn't the only one available. Several more badges are described below and all of them

carry the same four advantages in terms of social justification. These badges are termed *chronic* social justifications
because they are continually used for almost all types of inappropriate behavior.

## NEUROTICS

Most of us know people who proudly wear the badge of the
neurotic. Outrageous behavior is their keystone. Sometimes
these people openly flaunt their badge as a warning that they
are going to behave inappropriately and that we shouldn't
hold them accountable. It is interesting to note that one of
the functions served by psychiatrists and other professional
therapists is to validate their clients' use of the badge of the
neurotic. In a sense, these psychotherapists serve as the
manufacturers and licensed salespeople of these badges.

Neurotic badge wearers are usually a little more subtle
at social justification than alcoholics. Seldom will they just
come out and say, "Well, what can you expect from a
neurotic?" Instead, they'll hint at this conclusion by saying,
"I've just been so overwhelmed by anxiety the last couple
of days," and perhaps add a touch of legitimacy with, "My
therapist says I should act out my anxiety, but I don't think
either my friends or myself can tolerate that." Or, to use
the current terminology, the neurotic who has just failed to
keep an appointment will say, "Oh I don't know what I'm
going to do. I just can't seem to get it together to function
normally." Another favorite of neurotics is to justify inappropriate behavior on the grounds that their emotions keep
getting in the way of living up to everyday standards. A typical line might be, "I guess I'm just too *sensitive*, but I really feel things, and that affects the way I think and act."

People who wear the badge of the neurotic are fond of

justifications which serve to vindicate themselves and also attack the person who has disapproved of them. For example, Joan has spent most of the day in bed. Her husband, Chris, comes home expecting Joan to live up to her promise to get out of bed today and get some housework done. Chris sees the house in disarray and goes into the bedroom with a perplexed and slightly angry expression on his face. Before Chris can verbalize his anger and disapproval, Joan says, "Please don't say anything. You know that in my condition I'll just get more depressed." Or she may say, "Look, you know that my ego is weak and that my condition just gets worse when I sense that you don't love me." The last one is a real killer: Joan justifies on the grounds of her neurotic condition, plus she stops Chris from criticizing her and implies that his anger is an indication that he doesn't love her.

Neurotics, therefore, use the badge as a constant social justification and as a way to avoid responsibilities. Plus they have their defenders. When other people justify for them, they'll do so by citing some of the neurotics' good points: "You have to understand him. He's just really been nervous lately. He has a fantastic mind and is very creative when he's got his act together." All of this is not to say that neurotics have an easy life, but merely to point out that they do derive some benefits from this label.

## PHYSICAL ILLNESS

People can sometimes make an ailment last a lifetime and thereby continually use it to justify their failures. This illness may be quite real and actually debilitating, but many times the person will act as though the ailment is more severe or more frequently troublesome than it really is. Also, the person who does use an illness or injury as a badge for social justification will not acknowledge that there are others with the same or even worse affliction who do not use their infirmity as a justification for their failings.

Some people who do have legitimate illnesses or injuries may, at times, overuse them as excuses for justifying their behavior. More insidious, however, are people who use this badge by claiming an illness which is definitely untreatable by current medical science and often undiagnosable. Migraine headaches, back injuries, and irregularities of the circulatory system can usually work here.

People who do use the physical illness badge as a chronic social justification invoke it most frequently to avoid doing many of those things that are routinely expected of them. There are many social occasions which are downright boring. The physical illness badge wearer will avoid these situations on the grounds that, "I just don't feel up to it today. My back is killing me."

There are standards for behavior that proscribe certain actions, and there are other standards which prescribe that certain actions should be done. It is these latter standards which physical illness badge wearers will constantly violate and justify with their badges. For example, a husband says to his wife, "With my head thumping the way it is, I just don't feel I can go to visit your relatives tonight"; or "My back was bothering me so much today that I just couldn't get out to do any shopping"; or "I don't think I should go to the party tonight because I will probably get excited and my heart will act up." Students find this badge very convenient to use at test time.

The physical illness badge has a distinct advantage over the alcoholic or neurotic badge. In our society, a physical illness is customarily defined as a more legitimate justification than is a mental failing. Neuroticism and alcoholism are often seen as being somewhat under the control of the individual, but a physical illness or injury is seen as totally outside an individual's control. Therefore, a person is more likely to be exonerated from failing to attend a party if he claims a physical illness than if he says he simply didn't *want* to go. The physical illness badge, therefore, offers the same advantages that the alcoholic and neurotic badges confer, but it has the additional aura of medical legitimacy.

## RELATIVES

Another popular chronic social justification involves a badge which says "What can you expect from someone with relatives like mine?" A husband will justify his failure to live up to social obligations on the grounds that he is distracted, depressed, or exhausted because of his wife. Similarly, a wife will use the same kind of justification, except she implicates her husband. The cause of this burden may be the spouse's physical problems or mental condition. People who wear this badge act as though they are, or at least would be, okay people if it weren't for their burdensome spouses. It is easy, however, to get the impression that if the supposed yoke were removed, then these badge wearers would actually be lost. They would still behave inappropriately, but would no longer have their chronic social justification.

Of course, it doesn't have to be a spouse—almost any relative can be used in this way. A woman may continually complain that her children have been driving her crazy lately. Or, a man may repeatedly justify on the grounds that his aged parents are a constant worry. Some people even invoke an aging aunt or uncle who is "a constant source of strain." Usually when people invoke this badge they do so in terms of relatives they are trying to cope with at the present time. However, it is also possible to invoke this badge by citing problems with relatives from the past.

Psychoanalytic theory has given credence to the notion that certain early childhood experiences can cause serious problems in adulthood. Using this thesis, people claim to be permanently disabled because of treatment they received as children. Thus, someone who engages in excesses of sexual activity, drinking, or gambling will repeatedly justify this inappropriate behavior by saying, "I just can't help it. My parents were so authoritarian and restrictive that they never let me do anything." Or a person who acts selfishly will assert that this results from the fact that she was an only child, or that she came from a large family.

Another favorite justification involving parents is the plaintive cry, "My mother (or father) never really loved me." People who use this badge will invoke the supposed lack of parental love to explain virtually any inappropriate behavior, but they use it most consistently to explain why they themselves can't trust and love other people. Imagine Marsha and John are having a subdued argument about why Marsha isn't more affectionate. John accuses her of holding back on her feelings, and simultaneously encouraging him to become more committed to her. John levels several attacks on Marsha's honesty and sincerity, and then Marsha pulls out her badge: "You know I have trouble giving love because I fear rejection. I have my mother to thank for that. I loved her, but she never returned my affection."

The "My mother never loved me" badge offers, at best, a questionable defense; especially when we realize the sizable number of people who function quite normally even though their early home life was an emotional disaster.


I'M ONLY A CHILD

In general, children are not expected to conform to all of the standards for behavior applicable to adults. Children are routinely exempted from standards and negative character judgments on the grounds that they are, after all, "only children." And, since childhood does carry with it a very legitimate chronic social justification badge, many people are reluctant to surrender it. During the late teen-age years, early twenties, and in some cases even longer, people continue to socially justify on the grounds that they are "only a child." Such a badge is most effectively used with one's own parents.

The holder of the only-a-child badge is generally allowed to act very confused, erratic, and inconsistent, and to make decisions which are both socially and morally inappropriate. For example, Fran misses the final exam in a class, and on the date of the make-up exam she leaves for home. When she gets there and explains the situation, her parents get visibly upset with her actions. At that point Fran flashes her badge with a statement such as, "You know I can't cope with all these pressures, demands, and structures." If the parents are into this game, they'll clutch Fran and tell her that "it's all right," and that they'll "work something out." With a darling, little-girl smile Fran then says, "Oh, I feel so much better."

Even though the only-a-child badge holders must eventually leave home, it is sometimes possible for them to find a spouse or lover who will serve the function of the protective and reinforcing parent. In fact, in some relationships the partners are able to switch back and forth between the parent and child roles.

## MINORITIES

"I come from a deprived background." "My culture is different from yours." "It's just my feminine conditioning."

Statements such as these are examples of the kinds of social justifications used by people who wear the minority badge. This, of course, is not meant to imply that all minority members wear this badge, or that there have not been very real abuses which have influenced the behavior of minority members. It is the very fact that there is a note of legitimacy that makes this badge work. But the people who use this as an all-purpose badge tend to abuse it.

The minorities badge works best as a justification with people who are not members of the same minority. Blacks can use their minority status to justify their inappropriate behavior to whites, but seldom can they use it as successfully with other blacks. Similarly, the "only a woman" works better as an all-purpose badge with men than with other women.

The fact that other members of the same minority will not accept the minorities badge as a sufficient social justification is a reflection on the validity of this badge. People who are unaware of the extent to which the experience of being a member of a particular minority can affect an individual's behavior are frequently more willing to accept the minority badge as a justification. Members of the same minority are unlikely to accept it because they know that many people in their minority group function in a perfectly normal way. Further, on those occasions on which the minority badge is legitimately applicable, fellow members of the minority immediately realize this and it isn't even necessary for the other individual to show his badge.

## IF NOT A BADGE, THEN A BUTTON

If you are unwilling to pay the price of an all-purpose badge, then perhaps you'd be interested in something a little smaller. Say something you could always use in justifying certain specific *types* of inappropriate behavior. For example, do you have trouble keeping a checkbook accurate and up-to-date? Well, when criticized, simply say, "You know I'm just no good at math." Or if you are confronted for failing to send a birthday card to Aunt Mary, you respond by saying, "I can never remember things like that." Or after failing to fix some household appliance just admit, "I never did have any mechanical ability." In a similar way, if you seem always to be going the wrong way on one-way streets, turning left when you should have turned right, and generally just getting lost, then you should have no trouble saying, "You know I don't have any sense of direction."

As these examples indicate, the buttons approach involves the admission of a deficiency in a very specific ability. We admit to a deficiency in a particular area which is sufficient to justify a mistake, but which does not significantly lower our overall social worth. Society has even provided a few legitimate buttons. Claiming the role of artist or the profession of psychologist justifies acting a little crazy. These people still have to balance their checkbooks, but they can act foolish while doing it.

The badge justification involves admitting to possessing an undesirable characteristic. This admission may lower the individual's general social esteem to a certain degree, but not so much that he is categorized as socially unacceptable. In fact, by admitting a deficiency, the individual acquires a sort of legitimate social justification for almost any inappropriate action. The individual also, in a sense, gets a license to behave inconsiderately, and is excused from many responsibilities. And, since the individual repeatedly uses this same social justification, many of his colleagues will offer his justification for him.

# III

# SHOULD WE DO IT?

# 11

# Power, Power, Who's Got the Power?

## *Assessing the Alternatives and Their Consequences*

Up until this point we have taken social justifications at their face value, examining and interpreting them in terms of their specific content and what they say about us (e.g., we're honest, smart, sorry, etc.). But at a more general level these justifications contain additional messages. These messages go beyond the level of content and say something about our relationship with the other person and about how we view this relationship. At this general level all that matters is whether or not we gave a justification, and whether or not we did is a reflection of the nature of our interpersonal relationships.

Earlier it was pointed out that one of the major factors that determines whether or not we justify is how we feel about the observer. In other words, do we care if another person likes us or not? By implication, the fact that we justify to someone, regardless of the content or type of justification, indicates that, to some extent, we *do* care about the other person's opinion of us. Simply by expending the energy to justify, we are implicitly saying, "I want you to like me, because I like you."

At first glance, the justification and its implicit message may not seem all that powerful. After all, "I like you" is hardly anything earthshaking—we hear it every day. But imagine how you would feel if people stopped saying it to you, not only manifestly, but implicitly through their justifications. In all probability you would feel "hurt" and "rejected" and plagued by "self-doubt." There are many people who do find it difficult to openly say "I like you," or, conversely, to openly express their hostility. So for these people the giving and not giving of justifications becomes a primary means of communicating their love and anger. For example, if a husband is angry at his wife, he may indirectly communicate this feeling by not justifying (after, of course, creating the situation which under normal circumstances would have demanded a justification, like coming home for dinner an hour late). The wife asks where he has been and gets no answer. She will understand this not-so-subtle message, "You've made me mad, and—for the moment, at least—I don't like you." Should the wife get angry? Ignore the whole thing? Ask "what's wrong, John"? Apologize and beg forgiveness? Whatever her approach, you can be sure that once the situation gets back to normal and the husband has been pacified, he'll revert to his habit of justifying his misdeeds. (In fact, he'll probably justify his earlier failure to justify; "I'm sorry, but I was so mad that . . .")

Expressing liking for people is certainly nice, and the world could surely use more liking and niceness, but is that the primary message of our justifications? In Chapter 3, the point was made that the basic reason we like people— more basic than "I want you to like me"—is because of the rewards they can give us. To quell the rising chorus of "That may be true about other people, but it's not true about me!" let it be allowed that while it may not always be true, it is generally the case that the people we like best are the ones who can give us the most. Further, the reason we want to avoid people's disapproval stems from the fear that because they dislike us they may deny us their favors or even potentially cause us harm. Thus the element of dependency enters into our relationships, assuming a position of major significance.

Dependency, in turn, brings with it another major element—power. We have power over the people who are dependent upon us; likewise the people upon whom we are dependent have power over us. Our justifications serve to acknowledge these power hierarchies. If someone has power over us (can help or harm us, give or deny), we want to make certain that that person likes us, so we justify our failings, our misdeeds, sometimes even our very personality (because "I like you, and I want you to like me"). On the other hand, if the person doesn't have any power over us (can't really harm us), then we are less concerned about his opinions and feelings about us and are much less likely to justify ("I don't really care whether you like me or not"). To justify acknowledges another person's power and indicates our dependence; not to justify signifies our own power and proclaims our independence.

The importance of this power-conveying message is apparent in many everyday situations. One of the common signs of power is to be able to ask (preferably in a loud, accusatory voice) "Why did you do that?!" and to get a prompt, civilized, and submissive answer. Most employees are familiar with the type of boss who is always finding fault—with any and everything—and therefore demanding justifications. (Often this kind of character also wants to be thanked for pointing out our errors.) Workers quickly learn the ritualistic nature of many of these little exchanges, and realize that it is just a way for the boss to satisfy his need to feel superior and in control. If the employee doesn't realize this and doesn't justify, thereby demonstrating "who's boss," there will likely be much gnashing of teeth and a pink slip.

Many people who perceive themselves as being in positions of power, and, in fact, by traditional definition do have power (e.g., employers, supervisors, police officers, doctors, teachers, and—yes—men), seem to need a constant flow of information—and reinforcement—about their "power" position. If we give them an indication that we acknowledge their power by justifying, then usually they are quite happy. In fact, these people are sometimes so consumed with their own importance and power that they sincerely don't care what other people do. Thus, if we occasionally act as though we recognize their power by humbling ourselves with a social justification or two, they will frequently let us do whatever we want. These people seem to be attuned only to the implications of power implicit in the *form* of the behavior as opposed to its *content* (i.e., lots of pomp, but little circumstance). They appear to view all behavior in terms of power in interpersonal relationships and are acutely aware that social justifications are indicative of power. (They probably justify a lot to their own superiors.)

So by justifying to them, we provide reassurance of their position of power and authority.

It is obvious, then, that within interpersonal relationships that are characterized by a great deal of structure, social justifications are of great importance. And, since many of these power and authority hierarchies are so fragile and artificial, they must constantly be reinforced and reaffirmed—thus social justifications, which subtly and sometimes blatantly serve to constantly validate existing power relations. Behavior which deviates from the rules and standards established for the particular hierarchy is *quickly* and *thoroughly* justified so that no one needs to fear that the structure is in jeopardy. In other words, social justifications also are used to validate and maintain the status quo, which is especially important given the preponderance of relationships characterized by highly structured standards for behavior. When we socially justify, we let the other people know that our inappropriate actions are only unfortunate— and temporary—aberrations, and that in the future they can expect us to follow the rules. By doing this we decrease any uncertainty they might feel about "what to expect," and we reaffirm that the power structure and its accompanying rules for behavior are still intact. And, since there are so many possible deviations from the rules and since we always seem to be doing something inappropriate, social justifications are not only "important" in these relationships, they are absolutely "necessary."

One important implication of the idea that the greater a person's importance—or power—the greater is the likelihood that we will justify to that person is that it should be possible to determine how much power a person has in a particular situation by the number of justifications received or given. Thus, if you were with a new group of people and wanted to determine which one exerted the greatest influence, you would probably be safe in guessing that the individual who seldom justifies is the leader, and those doing the justifying are the followers. Similarly, if you wanted to determine your own standing in a particular group (work, family, or social), you could generally do so by assessing how often you justified relative to the frequency of justifications offered by the people around you. In general, the more time you spend justifying, the less time you spend in control. Only occasionally, when they really want something, will justifications be given by those people in positions of power. If it becomes too frequent an occurrence, these people jeopardize their standing in the power hierarchy.

This relationship between justification and power is apparent in nearly all situations. For example, in offices or factories, if the supervisors really have effective power, they will seldom justify, and instead will merely evaluate and listen to the justifications of the workers. The more tyrannical the supervisor, the more frequently the underlings will have to justify. (The tyrannical boss, of course, is something of a cartoon caricature—think of Mr. Dithers screaming at Dagwood Bumstead in the *Blondie* comic strip—but whether it is a case of art copying life or vice versa, in the real world of power hierarchies, THE BOSS does indeed exist.)

Similarly, in the school or classroom situation it is the students and not the teachers or administrators who must account for their actions. Students must justify tardiness, preparedness, physical appearance, and myriad other indiscretions, but teachers need justify nothing. Teachers routinely ask, "Why is your performance so poor, Freddy?" But the Freddies never get to ask, "Why are you such a poor teacher, Mr. Smith?"

This same relationship between a person's power and his frequency of justification is also readily apparent around the home. The most obvious example of this is the traditional relationship between parents and children. Children are asked, "Why did you do that?" so many times each day that it is no wonder they finally abandon specific justifications ("But Daddy, I didn't mean to . . ."; "But Mommy, I thought you meant . . ."), and shift instead to the all-purpose "I dunno." In the power hierarchy of the home, parents are relatively immune from the need to justify to their children. True, parental policy decisions are often challenged by children ("But why do I have to go to bed now/ eat that/wash my hands"), but none of these protests really challenge the basic parent/child power hierarchy. And when it is seriously challenged—perhaps when the "child" is 19 or 20 years old—the result is usually that the child leaves home amid recriminations and threats of disinheritance.

The power relationship between adults at home isn't quite as clear-cut as it is between parent and child. The stereotypical situation has the man in the seat of power and the "little woman" in the subservient role. Today, however, such stereotypes have little validity (if, in fact, they ever did). More typical today is the situation in which both spouses share the decision making; as a result, the power hierarchy is more a factor of how openly and often they display their power to others and the number of spheres in which they have power (i.e., he's in charge of the car; she handles the investments; she makes food and clothing decisions; he balances the budget). But who has the power is not the issue here. Rather, the point is that whichever person has power in the particular situation, the other will do the justifying. If the situation changes and the balance of power between the two reverses, so too will the frequency of justification.

It can be safely concluded that whatever the particular power structure, the mere existence of the structure itself will ensure the need to justify by one or several parties. And to the extent that there is a high frequency of social justification in a relationship, then power, and power struggles, are major elements in the relationship. Many idealistic people feel that power should not be a central aspect of interpersonal relationships—especially romantic ones. But when analyzed in terms of social justification—and the frequency thereof—it is nearly always the case that a great deal of power is involved, even (and sometimes most especially) in relationships that are said to be based primarily on "love." (How to structure these relationships and to integrate acts of justification into them will be discussed in the next chapter.)

The lesson to be learned from an awareness of the power hierarchy and the part that justifications play in determining its structure is that if a person wants more power, then he should stop justifying so much. In other words, this idea that the more power you have, the less you justify represents a handy guide on how to create the image of being powerful and how to avoid seeming weak and insignificant.

Specifically, it is suggested that in those situations (or relationships) in which we want to increase our power and be treated with respect and authority, we should demand justifications from others, but not respond to their demands that we justify. This means that we must demonstrate our disapproval of the behaviors of those we want to dominate, and whether we openly verbalize this disapproval ("Why did you do that?") or communicate it more discreetly (the cold stare), it must be obvious to all. Further, we must not only get others to justify, we must occasionally reject their justifications ("I simply don't believe you"), so that they will have to scrape around for something more convincing. Conversely, when one of these people dares to criticize our behavior, it is better—solely in terms of power—to either ignore their comments, or to point out to them that what *they* think has little relevance, and if they don't like it then they can "lump it."

The role that the giving and receiving of justifications plays in the indication of power in interpersonal relationships often goes unnoticed by people who are new to the arena of power. People just entering the business world and young people in general frequently act as though the way to get respect and authority is to "be nice" and to explain their every action. Being "agreeable" is a good way to get along with others, of course, but constant "niceness" and excessive justifications typically are interpreted as a sign of weakness by more experienced power players.

To illustrate the apparent logic beneath these interpretations, let's examine the case of someone who nervously laughs after expressing every opinion. What a nervous laugh generally indicates is that a person is not comfortable in the particular situation. In turn, this lack of comfort is assumed to mean that the person isn't really sure of himself, or, in other words, isn't confident of his power in relation to others. Some people might go so far as to say that this lack of confidence further indicates that the person doesn't really like himself. While this latter inference is perhaps unnecessary and excessive, the general idea that a nervous laugh indicates a position of low power is certainly valid. The image of the giddy teen-ager, giggling nervously after every comment, typifies this idea in the extreme.

In sum, people who are interested in being respected and taken seriously would be well-advised to reduce the numbers of their justifications. Keep in mind, however, that while reducing justifications will not automatically guarantee the immediate acquisition of power and a position of great esteem, the too-frequent use of justifications virtually ensures lower status in interpersonal relationships and an overall position of low power.

To counter these assertions that social justifications are part of elaborate power plays, some people may assert that they justify simply out of politeness. It is their desire to be polite that leads them to explain what they are going to do, or why they did what they did. After all, being polite is supposedly only "simple decency" and "common courtesy." While not denying politeness its status as a "nice thing to do" and even its expediency in many situations, it still seems useful to play the devil's advocate and suggest a look below the surface to understand exactly what is involved in "being polite."

To understand why we are polite, it might be useful to look at what would happen to us if we weren't polite, even though the situation obviously called for it. One consequence would be that people would get "the wrong impression." They would probably think that we were "impolite" and might very well tell other people. And that would be terrible, because all these other people would dislike us. This consequence brings us back to a familiar point—to avoid being disliked, we justify.

Another consequence of being impolite is that there "might be a misunderstanding." That's a lovely phrase, but what exactly does it mean? *What* might get misunderstood? Well, possibly someone might misunderstand what our motives were for doing something—someone might think that our intentions were "less than admirable." And the most likely consequence of that would be that the person would lower his esteem for us because we appeared to be untrustworthy—or simply unworthy. Another way of saying this is that people "might draw the wrong conclusion." Obviously this "wrong conclusion" is that we aren't as good as they had believed.

Another consequence of being impolite is that it would be "disrespectful of the other person." And this disrespect might, in turn, "hurt the other person's feelings," and he might very well "get angry" at us for hurting his feelings. His anger, a potentially undesirable consequence, is certainly something we would want to avoid. But while being polite to avoid someone's anger is certainly reasonable, it's quite a different thing from saying that we're polite out of "simple decency."

Since looking at the consequences of acting impolite keeps leading us to the same conclusion, perhaps we should look at the other side of politeness and examine the consequences of being polite. The primary result is that other people who also say that they value politeness would be "happy" and, as a consequence, would like us. They'd be "happy" because we were "so nice" (i.e., we seem to operate according to the same standards they do, so they know how to predict and control our behavior), and we'd be happy because we did something "nice" (we'd feel confident that since these people like us, then other people will too, and since other people control things we want, if we can get them to like us, we'll be able to get the things we need, and if we can get the things we need, then life will work out just fine). Of course, none of us has ever gone through this chain of logic while holding open a door, or while giving someone a seat on a bus, or even while justifying some "mistake" or errant behavior, nor should we delay opening the door or yielding our seat just to think through our motives. But they *are* there, and just being aware of them can help us in our interpersonal relationships.

To summarize this analysis of politeness, it seems that the most basic answer to why we value being polite is that *not* being polite would anger and displease others, while being polite will help us get along with others. In neither case, however, does "being polite" have anything to do with being inherently "good." This idea, that our reasons for being polite are rooted in self-concern and our own fight for survival, does not mean, of course, that being polite is "bad"—in fact, being polite is often more than just "nice," it's necessary. What this analysis *does* imply is simply that the idea of politeness for politeness' sake doesn't reveal the whole truth behind what we do. Returning to social justifications, the point is that we don't justify—or do polite things—simply out of a sense of decency, but rather because we want to avoid the disapproval of others.

Actually, this implication shouldn't really be all that surprising *or* offensive. All of us have observed others who are polite to those people who have power over them, while not being so conscientious around people without that power. And, while we might claim initially that we're not like that, the people who know us best would probably tell us (if forced) that we too are "occasionally" a little nicer to people whose favor we want and need than we are to the average or less-than-average schnook. Of course, in our case we are doing it because we are being forced to—politics, of course. Well, maybe those people we have observed are only doing what they're doing because they too have been "forced"—politics again, of course.

Perhaps the best way to summarize and conclude this entire thorny discussion would be to spell out the meaning of "politics." In this interpersonal context it means that other people are important because they control things we want or need—in other words, they have power over us. And if we are going to get these things, then we're going to have to make sure that they like us, and the best way to do this is to avoid giving them any reason to dislike us. Therefore, as was stated at the beginning of this chapter, we justify to affirm the superior position of people with power over us.

# 12

# The Fly in the Caviar

*The Disadvantages
of Justifying, Explaining,
and Otherwise Lying*

Let's face it! None of us is perfect! Yet by continually justifying, we act as though we were candidates for sainthood. We seem to operate on the assumption that if others discovered we had some faults it would be disasterous. To get a perspective on ourselves and on the discussion that follows about why we shouldn't justify, just try imagining the following:

Imagine that you are the parent of a child who is physically handicapped or who has some serious affliction. Your child seems to fluctuate between two basic approaches to life, and you want to guide him in selecting one of the two: (1) he stays home most of the time, and when forced to go out in public he immediately points out his disability, apologizes for it, and then slinks into a corner; (2) he takes part in all activites allowed within his physical limitations, and when he meets new people he doesn't make a big deal of his condition, nor does he in any way apologize for the limits on his activity.

Given the choice, surely all of us would choose the second approach and urge our child to participate in life as much as possible, and to do so in a straightforward, confident, and optimistic way. We know that there is no need for him to apologize because he may be physically different from others. In fact, we'd want him to forget and ignore— as much as possible—his supposed limitations. He's a person, and that's all that counts. Sure, he has some limitations, but who doesn't? It may take a little longer, and require more effort and ingenuity, but he can do many, many things.

If we feel this way about our child, why should we feel any differently about ourselves? Yet we do feel differently. We don't think our child should justify, but we think we should. What makes us different? Sure, we have some faults, and no doubt we're going to continue to occasionally blunder and to act inappropriately. But just as we wouldn't want our handicapped child to justify and apologize after his every error or mistep, we shouldn't allow ourselves to do so either. Our fallibility is always going to be there, and so will everyone else's. Instead of simply doing those many things we do well, however, we continually justify, and thereby give undue importance and emphasis to our limitations.

Since the major negative consequences of continual justification were presented in Chapter 1, they will be only briefly reviewed here, with the addition of a few that hopefully will have become more meaningful in the intervening chapters. By assuming that it really does matter to us that others are passing judgment on our every action, we are obliged to be self-conscious of our behavior. The result of this continual self-consciousness is that we tend to remove ourselves from those things that are most immediate. We don't react spontaneously, nor do we open ourselves to fully sensing and experiencing our present situation. It's as though we had on blinders and were only able to see the potential criticism our actions might earn us. Our self-consciousness interferes and we act with hesitance.

This defensive posture and its associated paranoia is based on a low level—but unrelenting—sense of anxiety. Most of us have adapted to this continual tension, and are even able to deny its existence until . . . . Until we remember those rare but wonderful times when we've been completely at ease because we felt we were completely accepted by someone. Until we remember the relief of truly "getting away" (maybe a vacation), away from the "normal demands" of our stress-filled lives.

Because these "escapes" *are* so very rare, the only way we have to cope with our anxiety is to try to stay in the world's good graces—by being "good," giving honest justifications whenever possible, and fabricating excuses when necessary. These lies, the criticism of ourselves and others, and the continual self-consciousness give rise to self-doubts and uncertainty about our own worth. It is painful, and it is a pain familiar to all of us.

Another basis of our feelings of self-doubt—perhaps the most important one—is that we wonder how we could ever have been so stupid as to get trapped in this mess, following a lifestyle in which we must always doubt ourselves,

worry about our actions, and justify. Despite our public pro-
testations that others have forced us to live this way, we
know that we are ultimately responsible. Every time we
offer a social justification we give up a part of our freedom.
We implicitly give the other person the right to judge us and
to publicly disapprove of us. The cumulative effect of regularly giving others the right to pass judgment on us is a substantial reduction of our freedom.

It is more or less assumed in our society that virtually
everyone has the right to pass judgment on the appropriateness of anybody's actions. This "right" is manifested
thousands of times each day in the frowns and grimaces of
the people we pass in review. The fact is undeniable: People
are constantly criticizing *and* being criticized. Gossip
magazines and columns feed on this criticism. One need
only read the kinds of questions asked Dear Abby to see
how involved we are in criticizing and in worrying about
what others think of us. Even the strangers on the street are
not free of our critical scrutiny, although in all probability
we will never see them again. Of what importance is
another person's walk, talk, or style? So what does it matter
that a woman's skirt is unfashionably short and that a man
stares at what is thereby revealed? What difference does any
of it make to us? None, absolutely none. The world isn't
going to stop spinning any time soon, but even if it were,
our frowns and criticisms of the behavior of the strangers
who inhabit it certainly wouldn't make any difference. Be
realistic—most of those people aren't relevant to you. There
may be no harm in looking at strangers, but few of us can
stop there—we must also evaluate them. But why do it?
Why restrict the freedom of others by passing judgment on
them? And why let so many of them pass judgment on us?

While it may seem to be part of the democratic tradi-
tion and some kind of ideal of freedom to let people pass

judgment on us, it doesn't have to be that way. There are, of course, some jobs and public situations where an individual's actions have a direct and real effect on others—in these cases it is necessary for the individual to be scrutinized and held accountable. In most everyday situations, however, such judgments not only aren't necessary, but actually function as infringements. What is involved here is a basic right—the right to be "ourselves" so long as we do not interfere with the rights of others. There is no way, of course, to prevent someone from mentally criticizing our actions and the even more minor things, like the clothes we wear. People can make judgments in their head if they want to, but that doesn't give them the right to openly express these judgments whenever they feel like it. That is a right we don't have to grant them.

By implicitly giving people the right to express their judgments, we get caught in the trap of social justification. We give them this right by not telling them to stop everytime they start to express a judgment of us. ("Stop. I don't want to hear. I really don't care what you think of my puce velour gaucho pants.") We get seduced into giving them this right because the judgments they express intially are usually very positive and flattering. ("Thank you. I think the page boy cut is very becoming to me too.") In listening to—and allowing—their praise, we are making ourselves a legitimate target for their later criticism.

We further compound our error of getting caught in the justification trap by expecting and often demanding justifications from others. And what is our explanation for passing judgments and expecting justifications? Why, to help other people, of course. If we point out their errors, then they can begin to correct them. We will help them learn the "right way" to act. We're just helpful teachers.

But how helpful are we? As "teachers," we seem to

feel that our "students" are very poor learners. What other explanation is there for the fact that most of us have to repeatedly disapprove and point out the same mistakes? Is that helpful? By continually disapproving of the same action, it begins to seem as though we're motivated by a desire to criticize rather than a desire to help. Telling the person once or twice really should be enough; additional criticism won't produce any change. Be realistic, we aren't teaching, we're complaining. And to keep complaining isn't going to help. We either have to adjust to what we consider someone's inappropriate behavior, or try not to be around that person so much. If we really want to help the other person, we must learn to offer support and confidence—confidence that our friend can change.

But honestly, is any of this necessary? Do we really need to be teachers? Imagine yourself in the role of student, with a teacher who is always pointing out your mistakes, demanding justifications, and telling you—whether implicitly or explicitly—the right way to do things. That gets irritating pretty fast. Of course, sometimes we do want, and actually appreciate, criticism and advice. But to be continually criticized for the same thing is downright annoying. Most of us know when we do something inappropriate. We don't have to be told each time, and we're not going to change just because someone tells us. And neither is anyone else, and we know that too.

We don't really want to be "helpful teachers." What we want is to get power over the other person by catching him violating a standard and then making him squirm around while trying to come up with a satisfactory justification. By pointing out the other person's errors, we are able to make ourselves look better by comparison, thereby elevating our positions. (Many people have observed that we're most likely to criticize others when we dislike and/or doubt our own potential.) More importantly, by forcing the other person to justify, we get him to implicitly reaffirm our authority, power, and control. But beware—this power may well be only temporary, because the person we just criticized is sure to be on the lookout for our own inappropriate behaviors, and will retaliate whenever possible.

All this begins to be very depressing. We are continually justifying because we want to appear "nice" and thereby maintain or improve our social standing. We force others to justify because we just have to assert our power and make sure that certain people know they are lower on the totem pole than we are. When considering all of the disadvantages, and remembering the example of your imaginary child with the disability, doesn't the prospect of just stopping all this nonsense seem like an attractive goal? Sure it does. But realistically, eliminating justifications completely is probably impossible because some of the conditions of contemporary life virtually dictate that we justify in certain situations. What *is* possible, however, is to cut back, to dramatically reduce the amount of justifying we do.

The first step in this process is to determine the kinds of situations and relationships in which we can cut back. There are some situations involving "first impressions" in which social justifications do appear to be justifiable. There are times when first impressions really do count, and we can't afford to merely take the attitude, "If you are going to dislike me because of my one inappropriate action, then I don't want you as a friend." These types of first impression situations are relatively few in number, however, and they all have two important elements in common.

The two factors, *both* of which must be present before a social justification is justifiable, are: (1) the other person has real power over us, or at least the potential of such power, and (2) it is possible that if this person sufficiently dislikes us, then we will never see him or her again. "Real power" means that the other person's disliking must have direct material consequences for us, that it may substantially affect the quality of our lives (for example, not getting a job because the interviewer didn't like us).

If this person with power over us does dislike us on the basis of our inappropriate behavior, his disliking may mean that he won't give us what we want and additionally won't want to be around us anymore. In such a situation, one in which we have created an impression so negative that the other person will decide to avoid us, an adroit social justification seems reasonable and appropriate. If we are certain, however, that we *will* see the other person again, then we should not justify, regardless of the negative impression we may have created. By seeing us again, this person will be able to observe more of our behavior, and his overall impression of us will be based on these subsequent—and hopefully more "appropriate"—actions as well as the initial blunder. Too often we have the unrealistic fear that, because of one inappropriate act, other people are going to avoid us and try not to be in our presence. Typically the person won't avoid us, and often can't help but see us (e.g., a new neighbor, work associate, classmate). If we do possess good qualities, then they will see them over a period of time. To give in to our initial fear of rejection would lead us to justify in these first-impression situations, and as a result we would get trapped into yet another power game relationship, with all the attendant anxiety, scrutiny, and dishonesty.

These guidelines—that we should only justify when the other person both has power and may never see us again—can be translated into very practical terms. To do this, think of a continuum which begins with people we don't know at all and runs all the way to people with whom we are intimately involved. The stages are: strangers, acquaintances, associates, and true friends or intimates. To determine when and where on this continuum it is reasonable to justify, all we have to do is apply the two criteria to these four general types of relationships.

"Strangers" are, by definition, people we do not know and whom we are unlikely to ever be around again. And, because we're not going to be around them again, they seldom have any "real power" over us. If the mechanic, maitre d', and salesperson indicate that they don't like our looks or the way we are acting, then that's their problem. There's nothing they can do to us, and we can just take our business and affection elsewhere. So although we may never see a "stranger" again—which satisfies one of the criteria for justifying—strangers lack the "real power" over us which would also be necessary to make us justify. There are some apparent exceptions to this. Some "strangers" do have power over us. Typically, however, while they as individuals are "strangers," their professional identity is no stranger to us. We are speaking here of such persons as police officers, I.R.S. agents, court judges, personnel managers, and customs agents. Justifying our actions to these people is usually a wise and expedient thing to do, because they are invested with real power by the nature of their positions, and will use their power before we've had time to demonstrate our goodness.

"Acquaintances" are a bit more complicated. Even though we may not yet really know a particular person, we may have reason to believe that this person will be important to us. It is, therefore, hardly reasonable to call such a person a "stranger." Therefore, the next step on the continuum is to categorize such people as "acquaintances." Now, whether or not we ever see these people again may well depend on whether or not they like us (and we like them). Therefore, if we feel for any reason that this new acquaintance might be able to affect us materially (has power over us, or has potential for such power), then we would probably want to justify. In such a situation, both criteria would have been satisfied. If, however, we feel that this new acquaintance is somebody who would never have power over us, and we don't care if we ever see the person again, then we might well treat this person as a "stranger" and not justify.

For example, assume that a fellow you run into occasionally with friends, or at the cafeteria or the tennis courts, has gotten into the habit of frowning at one of your habits (e.g., boastful remarks and raucous laughter). You have several options. The first is, as a chronic justifier, you will apologize for whatever it is you're doing that he finds offensive (and play right into his hands by justifying every time he pushes your button). The second option is to let this fellow know that you don't care whether he approves of you or not, and that you are not going to justify. If he doesn't like it, he can just find another cafeteria and another cream puff. (This action, of course, assumes that the other person can in no way hold power over you, and serves also to burn a few bridges.) If, on the other hand, you do feel that this acquaintance just might have a direct influence on the quality of your life, then you would opt for a third course of action—you'd justify, but only selectively. If he holds potential power over you, and there is a real chance that your inappropriate behavior may cause him to never see you again, then justification is your only way out. Be careful, though—it is easy to be fooled (usually by fooling ourselves) about how vital someone is to our existence.

The case of "associates" (e.g., the people we work with) is slightly different than that of acquaintances. Typically (especially if they are peers) they don't seem to hold any power over us. And we certainly are going to be seeing them on a continual basis. So "associates" don't seem to qualify for justifications because they don't meet either of the two basic criteria. At least that's the "ideal" way to look at things. The more pragmatic view, however, is to acknowledge that they do have power and can make our life miserable in a hundred small ways every day. Their pettiness can be so irritating that every working day is a form of torture. The crucial factor here is the "forced" nature of our association. We can't escape from them or force them out of our lives. They'll be around the office for a long time to come, no doubt. We have no choice as to whether we associate with these people, and as a result we often compromise and act out the ritual of justification with them. Be aware, however, that by so doing you are giving up a lot of personal power, and that too may be detrimental.

By definition, "true friends" and people who know us "intimately" are people with whom we're going to have continuing contact. In almost all cases, these people have "real power" over us, but they also already know our faults and, by remaining friends, have tacitly agreed to live with and accept them. In these relationships, therefore, we can do a lot of cutting back on our justifications. This may at first seem a little strange—justify to people we hardly know, and skip it with those that we care most about. In a very real sense, however, by *not* justifying we are indicating just how much we trust and value these people. There is no need to be constantly on guard, to explain our every move, to worry about how these people view us. It is precisely because we want these relationships to be as good and as complete as possible that we want to eliminate the anxiety and pain of justification. We truly care about them, and unless their behavior becomes incredibly punishing to us (an unlikely event), we will always care about them. We accept the fact that they are less than perfect, and they accept our failings. Thus, with true friends we have a very real opportunity to stop or decrease our justifying—and by so doing we expand our acceptance and love.

To summarize, in general the types of relationships in which we can cut back on justifying are (1) those in which we don't know the other person very well (or at all) and don't care if we ever do; and (2) those cases in which we know the person very well and care a great deal. It is primarily in those relationships where our friendship is just developing that we probably will need and want to continue justifying.

When we think seriously about breaking the justification habit, most of us feel more than just a little nervous. We fear that our close friends will reject us, associates will actively work to harm us, acquaintances will cross the street to avoid us, and strangers will punch us in the nose. And it might in fact happen that way—but it shouldn't. Associates, acquaintances, and strangers are unpredictable people—if we decide to stop explaining ourselves and our actions to them, then we may encounter some hostility. But not with friends, or at least not with people who *really are* friends. Friends recognize our imperfections and accept us as we are, just as we know theirs' and love them anyway. Given this basic acceptance between true friends, it seems unreasonable to continually act as though our inappropriate actions could cause a serious misunderstanding. Rather, with friends we should be patient, hesitant to pass judgment, and open to the increased intimacy that can arise from a truly open and unemcumbered relationship.

# 13

# Not Having to Say "I'm Sorry"

## *Breaking the Habit*

Assuming that we have overcome any fears and are ready to experiment with breaking the habit of justifying, there are a few practical and easy things we can do. The essential first step to cutting back on the amount of justifying we do is to stop expecting other people to give justifications to us. The rationale behind this maneuver is that people respond to us in two ways: (1) they generally give us what we demand of them, and (2) they treat us the same way we treat them. Therefore, when others give us what we demand, they then feel free to expect us to give them what they demand. If we stop demanding justifications all the time, then people will have less reason for demanding them of us. It is surprising how quickly there will be a noticeable change in our relationships with others when we stop making this demand—in a very short time it will be apparent that others are more relaxed and comfortable with us, and we likewise will feel more at ease with them.

If we want to speed up this process, we can make a declaration, sincerely telling our friends that they don't have to justify to us, that we trust them and won't condemn them for their actions (or non-actions), that they truly don't need to say "I'm sorry" to us. Whether we make a declaratory statement or indicate through our actions that others need not justify to us, communicating this idea can be very difficult at first. Usually it requires explaining to other people just what social justifications are, pointing out that they are a form of lying—both to oneself and to others—and that they are usually unnecessary and a definite hindrance in developing close relationships with others.

This explanation, which probably will be greeted with stunned silence and a glimmer of disbelief, must be followed up with actual behavior, such as not asking people why they did things, and stopping others from giving their justifications. When they begin to justify, say something like, "It's okay, you don't have to explain to me," or "Look, I like you, and there is no reason for you to apologize." Expressions such as these, stated with sincerity and reinforced by the refusal to even listen to the justification, will usually be enough to start the process.

Firm resolve on our part and frequent reassurance to the people around us may, however, be necessary at first. Personal experience has shown that some people will persist in giving justifications despite our indication that it is neither necessary nor wanted. These persistent persons will say, "Yeah, okay, I know it's not necessary, but I just want to explain . . . ." As soon as that "but" comes out, we have to stop them. The most obvious course would be to issue an emphatic demand that they not "explain" anything. We may even resort to the dramatic child's technique of covering our ears and closing our eyes. Then we should patiently explain again that we feel our relationship is such that apologies and other justifications are unnecessary, that we intend to stop offering justifications ourselves, and that in fact we will like them less if they persist in showing so little faith in our relationship by constantly justifying.

The danger implicit in this bold approach, and something which should be avoided, is that this process of not offering social justifications can turn into a real tactic of one-upmanship and a personal power trip. It is very easy to communicate a sense of superiority, and it is very easy to feel superior when we have announced that we don't expect justifications, yet the others persist in offering them. First of all they are more or less "humbling" themselves to us, and secondly there is a tendency to radiate smug condescension in the "See-I'm-more-secure-than-you" attitude. When we allow this to happen *we* are the real losers. Our friends will become aware of the fact that they are being dishonestly manipulated and that behind our expressions of concern there is a great big power plot. So we must be careful how we go about this whole process, and be clear about our goal. We want to improve the relationship, not just our position.

Even the most persistent social justifier will stop if we effectively indicate several times that we honestly and sincerely don't expect or want any more explanations and apologies. Our expectations must be clearly and forcefully communicated, and always with respect. Remember, the person is justifying because he thinks we don't like him. So the crucial message to communicate is that "It's okay; I like you." If the other person still persists, then it is probably because he has a secret agenda of goals he wants to accomplish in the relationship, and it may be time to rethink our relationship with that person.

Now that we have decided that we are going to stop justifying, and we know that the first step is to stop expecting it from others, we must decide who to start stopping with. If you remember, there were four classifications of people: strangers, acquaintances, associates, and intimates. To begin the process of non-justification, it is best to begin with the two extremes—strangers and intimates.

In the case of strangers we need to spend some time monitoring our habits and actions and then select one situation (say, paying for a newspaper or a pack of gum with a ten dollar bill) in which we justify and would like to stop. This decided, the next time we're about to enter into this situation we have to remind ourselves that we are not going to justify ("Okay, kiddo, you just plop out the ten spot and brace yourself"). When you catch that first glance of disapproval, just flash a blank expression (do not feign innocence or sweetness and do not yield to the temptation to adopt a stance of haughty indifference). It takes a strong determination to get through the first few of these encounters. But persevere, it will be worth it.

Unfortunately, since we are dealing with strangers in these instances, there won't be anyone around to appreciate our accomplishment and to reward our efforts with the praise they deserve. (Unless, of course, we happen to be in line with a group of former justifying addicts who break into spontaneous applause.) When you get home, tell your sympathetic friends, because their praise and support will be very useful. It is beneficial to get an objective indication of success. Perhaps you'll want to keep a little score card, like people do on some smoke-ending programs, on which you can record your successes and failures.

Stopping the justifying habit with intimates—those people we are closest to and "care for" the most—can be somewhat more problematic than with strangers because it can put a real strain on the relationship if we are not very careful. As was explained earlier, the first step is to stop expecting justifications from the other person and to declare our intention to stop giving them as well. In an intimate relationship it is imperative that both parties be committed to breaking the habit (you don't get to walk away from intimates as you can with strangers). First we must establish a common understanding of the dynamics of social justification and the many forms these justifications can take. (Getting the other person to read this book would be a good start.) Next, pick out one or two specific types of justifications to work on first (e.g., nervous laughter, "you made me do it," redefinition, or "well, it could have been worse"). In making these selections, it's best for both persons to pick out one of the other's justifications he or she finds most annoying.

The greatest help each person can then provide is in shaping the other's behavior so that the frequency of justification is reduced. The rules by which this process will operate must then be established. The most tempting approach is to monitor the other person's behavior and condemn each apology, explanation, or general justification. ("Gotcha!" "You did it again!") Punishment is not nearly as effective, however, as praise. Each person should reward the other every time the temptation to justify is successfully resisted. This means being very alert to the other person's habits, so that we will be aware of the *absence* of the justification. Comments such as, "I'm glad you didn't justify that,"

"Thanks for not apologizing," and "Good boy," while they may seem totally inane on this printed page, do help to make it worthwhile in the actual situation for the person to stop justifying. Pay attention, and notice every time the person resists justifying. Immediately express your praise and gratitude.

Communicating this praise can be especially effective because it is sincere. It will be sincere because the other person has stopped doing something that grated on you. Remember, you picked out the most irksome of justifications for the other person to work on. Another reason this praise is sincere is that we can legitimately express thanks since the other person has indicated a great deal of trust in us. By not socially justifying, the other person has indicated that he has confidence in our feelings for him and confidence in our capacity to be mature, broadminded, and generous in judging and dealing with him. It means that we are trusted and are allowed to trust in return.

Inevitably there will be occasional lapses when the other person reverts to explaining or apologizing when it is no longer wanted or necessary. In those cases remember to be gentle. Don't become irritated or gloat over the inadvertent slip. To do so would be to revert to the old power game by creating the kind of authoritarian situation that the experiment is designed to eliminate. Besides, it won't help.

If anything, these lapses should be an occasion for laughter. We are funny because we try to act as though we can achieve perfection. We foolishly attempt to constantly convince ourselves and others that we have our world completely organized and under our control. Somehow we never seem to comprehend the obvious: we can't completely mold our actions or our world into a perfect system that is good, right, and true. But, we do keep trying.

Breaking the justification habit with the third category

of people—associates—is quite a bit more difficult than it is with strangers and intimates. It is relatively easy to stop justifying to strangers because we can just walk out of their lives: only in unique circumstances can they retaliate. With intimates we make the decision to stop justifying, we communicate this intention, and we can usually count on their cooperation. With associates you can't just walk away from them, nor can you count on their cooperation.

When we stop justifying to associates—or even if we announce our intention to stop—it is highly probable that one of these associates will complain and accuse us of being rude or unfeeling or selfish or uncooperative—all because we no longer want to explain the meaning of all our actions ("I didn't mean to step on your toe"; "I'm late because of traffic"). If we are really tenacious, and press them for the reasons why they always need some explanation or justification for our actions, they may respond, "I'm simply trying to understand you better." That's fine, but *why* do they want to understand us better? Could it be that they want to understand just for the sake of understanding (a motive hard to fault, and equally hard to believe)? Or could it be—as many people would say—that they only want to "know you better" so that they "can improve *our* relationship"? Or could it be that there's a little something in it for them?

Basically, in "understanding" us they are attempting to learn the "cause" of our actions. The reason they want to learn the cause is that they want to be able to predict how we will behave in the future. They assume that if the inappropriate behavior was due to our inconsiderateness or stemmed from our lack of ability, then chances are the offensive deeds will be repeated. If there was some outside influence, however, some intervening factor (i.e., a traffic jam, a sick friend, Blue Monday), that means that it is less likely to recur, and they are safe in associating with us. If

they "understand" us, then we are sufficiently "predicta-
ble," and therefore can be trusted to respond when our buttons are pushed. That means that, if necessary, we can be
"manipulated." Thus we are "trustworthy" and "safe" to
have around. Whether consciously or not, it all comes back
to the old power game: they want to understand us so that
they can protect themselves and guarantee that they will get
what they want.

If faced with such a situation, and with the awareness
that this associate is one that we have to get along with (or
at least that life will be more tolerable if we do), then
perhaps it is best to go ahead and justify. You say, "I'm
sorry; it won't happen again," even though you both know
it may very well happen again. Sometimes, no matter
whether you are really sorry or not, it's easier just to go
along with the rote expression of a justification. At the same
time, try not to revert to your old habits of continual justification. Do it selectively—and in as low a voice as possible.

The fourth category of people we encounter—the
acquaintances—are the most difficult to counsel on. They
are acquaintances only because we really don't know much
about them—they may prove to be important to us, or they
may quickly be strangers. Because of this somewhat nebu-
lous situation, it is best to proceed with caution, essentially
"playing it by ear." Don't offer any gratuitous justifications, but at the same time try not to burn your bridges.

The thought of actually succeeding at not justifying
may make some people envision hostility, ostracism, and
desertion (from your best friend, your spouse, or your dog),
while others foresee the gaining of considerable personal
power, status, and popularity. Well, both visions are potentially accurate—the resolution of the apparent contradiction
is simply the matter of time.

Be prepared. When you stop justifying, especially to

associates and strangers, they will use every device available to them to force you to justify. This attack may begin with a straightforward demand ("What did you mean by that?"). If that gets no response, then they may resort to irony ("I beg your pardon"), or anger ("Well! Who do you think you are?"). Subsequently you can expect all of the following: surprise ("!?!"); concern ("Was it something I did?"); sweetness ("You can tell me what's bothering you"); hurt ("You don't really care about me, do you?"); greviously offended ("You've got your nerve!"). All are merely efforts to cajole us into justifying. They will exert all of this effort because, by not justifying, we are negating some of the basic assumptions of our relationship with them. They interpret our action of not justifying as a declaration of independence and thereby view it as a challenge to their power. And no one is going to give up power without a fight—so be prepared to resist.

When people start applying this pressure on us, it no doubt will be tempting to capitulate to their demands. And we do, all the while insisting that we are not justifying, but rather that we are merely going to give them "an explanation." Bolstering this temptation to give "an explanation" is the idea that we are only going to tell them "the truth," and that our motive in explaining is only to "help the person to understand." Of course, under close cross-examination we probably would have to admit that the real reason we want them to understand is so that they won't get "the wrong impression" of us. And that "wrong impression" is that we are not very nice people, that we are socially unacceptable. So where does that put us? Isn't that goal, the reducing of the other person's disapproval, the very hallmark of a social justification? So be careful, or else in resisting the temptation to justify you will be seduced into giving its blood relative, the "explanation."

If you can maintain your resolve and resist these demands that you justify, you must then prepare yourself for an even more corrupting reaction. If you're successful, and are able to cut out all the unneccessary explanations and justifications, you will not only liberate yourself from a fantastic burden, but you will become the object of admiration and deference. Suddenly you will find that you have acquired new charisma. People who were accusing you of snobbery and arrogance will treat you with new-found awe and respect.

Such a reversal may seem unlikely, but it will happen. In fact, not only will you be admired, you will also be feared. People will view you as being totally self-confident, self-sufficient, and therefore virtually outside of their control. To most people, not justifying is a sign of great self-confidence, and by not justifying you are indicating to them that your happiness and your existence in no way depends on their liking you.

Obviously all of this deference, fear, and power can be very heady and—in the long run—even more destructive than the trap of social justification. Therefore, it is necessary to be certain of your goals when you stop justifying. If power is what you want, then have at it—but remember: it's reputedly very lonely at the top.

Let's take stock. We've decided that we want to stop justifying, but we are aware, too, of the many pitfalls and problems involved in breaking what is not only *our* habit, but one of everyone else around us. We are used to supplying justifications; they are used to receiving them. Of course, in some situations and relationships you may decide that it is extremely "useful" to justify. In such a case there is one justification that is both simple and reasonable. Remember that the other person is asking why we acted as we did (inappropriately) in order to better predict how we will act in the future. So if we really want to justify, the most courteous and efficient one to use is: "It won't happen again." By simply promising that we will improve in the future, we avoid the entanglement of speculation as to the possible causes of our errant action, and we give the questioner the final conclusions for which he is searching.

Of course, the other person many not be satisfied with the "It won't happen again" justification, instead preferring a greater display of deference, pain, and penitence on our part. If indeed that is being demanded of us, then it is clear that this relationship involves a full-scale power struggle. The "now-I've-got-you!" attitude implicit in demands for detailed emotional justification is indicative of continuing superior/inferior power positions.

On the other hand, the person who does accept our simple promise to improve is one who probably is more concerned with what can be produced from a relationship with us rather than with the dynamics of the relationship in and of itself.

There will, of course, be times when someone will question the appropriateness of our behavior and we simply won't be able to promise that we will improve or change. The honest answer may have to be "I may do that again from time to time," or "That's the way I am, and I don't think it or I will change." Either of these answers puts the other person in the position of having to decide whether the unpleasantness of our actions outweighs the importance and benefits of a relationship with us. The fact that we have given these answers, refusing to promise that we will mend our ways, implies that in fact we are more concerned with maintaining our own integrity than we are with maintaining our relationship with the other person. The resulting confrontations may be very unpleasant (after all, that's why we

like to avoid them by justifying), but quickly getting a resolution to such conflicts (even if the resolution is dissolution
of the relationship) is really the best approach.

Breaking the justification habit does not mean that we
are social rebels, that we don't want to act in accord with
all the many conventional norms. There is only one traditional rule that we are breaking: we don't want to justify, to
explain every time we violate a rule. We do value those
rules, and we will continue to subscribe to them and to live
up to them—all of them except the one that says that we
have to explain away, lie about, and apologize for all our
actions.

Breaking the justification habit also does not mean that
we are being impolite or inconsiderate of others. In fact, to
the extent that being polite means being helpful, decent, and
understanding, we will be just as polite, if not more so, than
in the past. By not asking for justifications from others we
are being very polite and considerate. By not demanding
explanations, we are attempting to create the kind of relationship in which everyone is given the benefit of the doubt
and no one immediately assumes the worse possible in-
terpretation of another person's actions (and errors). Such a
relationship is based on the kind of trust that politeness attempts to foster.

Additionally, breaking the justification habit does not
mean that we won't still open doors, say "thank you,"
"excuse me," or control our own selfish desires. It does
mean, however, that we refuse to be treated as virtual criminal defendents after every act someone views as a misdeed.
Although some may view our unwillingness to justify as
selfishness, it is at worst a selfishness which is harmless to
others. And that, by the strictest set of values, is not reprehensible.

What breaking the justification habit does mean is that we are able to extract ourselves from the burdens of coping with the power games inherent in most relationships. It also may mean the end of some relationships, but if it does, then it was the "wrong" relationship anyway.

Stated as simply as possible, the aim of reducing—or ideally, in eliminating—justifications is to unencumber our lives. It is like pruning a large tree: you cut off the smaller branches so that there will be more space and more nourishment for the growth of the stronger, more important limbs. Clearing away the impediment of justification, eliminating the lies and their snarling entanglements, will provide the additional space and energy necessary for the successful growth and maturation of our relationships and ourselves.